FOUR SEASONS PASTA

FOUR SEASONS PASTA

A Year of Inspired Recipes in the Italian Tradition

by **Janet Fletcher**

Photographs by Victoria Pearson

CHRONICLE BOOKS

SAN FRANCISCO

ACKNOWLEDGMENTS

No cookbook is a solo effort. Several people helped, advised, and encouraged me with this project, and I'd like to acknowledge them here. First, I'm indebted to Chronicle Books editor Bill LeBlond for immediately embracing this book idea. Photographer Victoria Pearson and stylist Christine Masterson have once again rendered my recipes with imagination and good taste. Chronicle Books designer Brett MacFadden created the book's distinctive look, and I am grateful for his flexibility and willingness to consider my input. Editorial assistants Amy Treadwell and Holly Burrows helped keep the book on track and were eagle-eyed in spotting inconsistencies. Carrie Bradley was a knowledgeable and sensitive copy editor, and I feel fortunate that this project ended up on her desk.

For assistance with content I'd like to thank Paula Wolfert, who let me roam in her splendid library; Arthur Schwartz and David Shalleck for correcting my Italian; and Rolando Beramendi and Carolyn Buck of Manicaretti for countless favors, large and small. Special thanks go to Nicolina Peduzzi, Gianluigi Peduzzi, and all the rest of the extended Peduzzi family who welcomed me into their Abruzzese home, shared their recipes and pasta expertise, and made me feel like another member of the family. Finally, mere thanks aren't enough for my good-natured husband and sous chef, Douglas Fletcher, who fortunately shares my enthusiasm for pasta.

Library of Congress Cataloging-in-Publication Data available.

ISBN 0-8118-3908-7

Designed by Brett MacFadden

Prop styling by Ann Johnstad
Food styling by Christine Masterson

Manufactured in China.

Distributed in Canada by Raincoast Books
9050 Shaughnessy Street
Vancouver, BC V6P 6E5

10 9 8 7 6 5 4 3 2 1

Chronicle Books LLC
85 Second Street
San Francisco, California 94105

www.chroniclebooks.com

TABLE OF CONTENTS

What's for dinner? At my house, on a typical weeknight, there's a good chance it's pasta with vegetables. If I could think of other dishes that were equally easy, healthful, quick, economical, and satisfying, I would make them—but I can't. In my estimation, it would be difficult to find a more sensible way to eat for life.

For convenience, I keep my kitchen stocked with the pasta basics: dried noodles, good olive oil, anchovies, capers, olives, canned tomatoes, and grating cheese. My own garden, neighborhood grocery, and local farmers' market provide the rest, a changing parade of vegetables for pasta sauces that follow the seasons.

It's impossible to grow bored when your pasta repertoire tracks the harvest. Just when you think you've had enough asparagus, they leave the stage, replaced by fava beans and peas. On the heels of the last tomatoes come the first autumn squashes, like the dense kabocha, perfect for stuffing ravioli. And when winter skies are grayest, the market fills with tempting pasta greens: mustard, broccoli rabe, cabbage, and kale.

From years of traveling in Italy, I know that many Italians share my passion, especially in the poorer south. In Puglia and Sicily, people eat pasta with vegetables daily, not because they are poor any longer, but because their communities once were and a regional taste for simplicity endures.

Orecchiette with broccoli rabe, the iconic dish of Puglia, could hardly be more humble. In times past, the broccoli rabe came from the household *orto,* or garden; the olive oil from a neighbor, probably in trade; the fresh orecchiette from the cook's hands, made with only semolina and water, no costly eggs. (Today, most Italian home cooks buy dried pasta.) For a pittance you had a nourishing meal, one that's still commonplace on Puglia's tables, and not just among the frugal. Even Italians of means take pleasure in these simple, seasonal dishes. I have eaten pasta with wild mustard greens at the table of a *marchesa.*

In the following pages, you'll find four seasons' worth of ideas for saucing pasta with fresh vegetables. Most of these recipes come from the Italian tradition, from dishes I've sampled in Italian restaurants and homes. A few are my own fantasies and incorporate vegetables I particularly love, such as fresh shelling beans. With the exception of the stuffed dishes—cannelloni and ravioli—the recipes are uncomplicated, easy to execute, and within the capabilities of beginning cooks.

Although I chose the sauces in this book because they showcase seasonal vegetables, the collection is not vegetarian. Many recipes include a little sausage, pancetta, prosciutto, or anchovy as an accent or enrichment, but vegetarians can simply leave them out. Those who make the recipes as written may be surprised at how satisfying a nearly meatless meal can be.

When entertaining, you can serve these dishes in small portions as a first course, followed, in the Italian style, by fish or meat. But as a daily matter, I enjoy these pasta preparations as a main course. When my husband and I dine alone, I make a half-recipe, supplemented by a few olives or toasted almonds to nibble on while we're cooking, and a salad or wedge of cheese afterward. If there's a better way to eat for long-term health and satisfaction, I don't know it.

A good sauce is nothing without good pasta underneath. For the best results, take some time to master the fundamentals of choosing dried pasta, making fresh pasta, and correctly cooking both. You'll find guidelines to these basic techniques in the following pages.

choosing pasta

The most significant step you can take in becoming a better pasta cook is to choose a good brand of dried pasta. Well-made pasta cooks to an evenly firm, al dente texture. It has a pleasant, wheaty flavor and a rough texture that encourages the sauce to adhere.

Inferior pasta is slippery. When boiled, it turns mushy outside before it's done inside. It has little wheaty taste and lacks the chewy elasticity of high-quality pasta, even when you take pains not to overcook it. Poorly made pasta can compromise the most carefully tended sauce, so it makes sense to insist on quality.

Superior pasta starts with high-quality durum wheat, typically blended from different sources to get a combination of flavor and strength. Manufacturers continually monitor their flour deliveries to make sure each batch has the low humidity and high protein content they want.

Beyond the flour, two other factors contribute significantly to quality: a long drying time at low temperatures, and the use of bronze dies. Inexpensive industrial pasta is dried in a few hours at high temperatures, which alters the protein characteristics and thus the flavor and texture of the pasta. More quality-conscious manufacturers may take 36 to 48 hours to dry their noodles, a costly practice but one that pays off by preserving taste and texture.

The dies are the disklike attachments used to cut the pasta into myriad shapes, from spaghetti to shells to wagon wheels. The better producers use heavy bronze dies, which yield a rough-textured pasta. But bronze dies are expensive and require frequent maintenance so more cost-conscious producers use Teflon dies. Pasta cut with a Teflon die is smooth and slick on the outside, so sauce doesn't cling well. You can feel the difference among shapes cut with bronze versus Teflon dies, and you can see it clearly with a magnifying lens.

Not surprisingly, good pasta costs more, but I think it's a price worth paying. Among supermarket brands, I think De Cecco is exceptional—a top-quality, affordable Italian pasta for everyday use. For guests or special occasions, I spring for the top-of-the-line Italian brands, such as Rustichella, Latini, and Martelli. I have yet to find a domestic pasta with the cooking and eating qualities I seek.

cooking pasta

Many myths persist about cooking pasta, and they turn up as questions whenever I teach a pasta class. Although the cooking process could hardly be simpler, people seem to want to make it complex. They worry about when to add salt to the water, whether to add oil, how to test for doneness, and how to keep noodles from sticking together.

You will cook perfect pasta every time if you follow these guidelines:
Use lots of water. Pasta needs to swim freely in rapidly boiling water to shed its starch and cook evenly. To cook 1 pound of pasta, I use an 8-quart pot filled with 6 quarts of salted water. Cooking pasta in too small a pot with too little water is the most frequent mistake I see others make.

Salt the water generously. The salt has nothing to do with helping the pasta cook faster, as some claim, and everything to do with flavor. Yes, salt raises the boiling point of water, but you would have to use a more-than-palatable amount to bring the boiling point up significantly. The salt's purpose is to flavor the pasta.

Many recipes insist that you salt the boiling water just before you add the pasta. I salt the water just after I fill the pot so I won't forget to do it. It makes absolutely no difference. Salt it whenever you like, as long as you do so before you add the pasta. Although I never measure, 2 tablespoons of salt to 6 quarts of water is about right.

Should you put oil in the pasta water to keep the noodles from sticking together? Definitely not, with one exception. Oil does prevent sticking, but it also keeps the sauce from clinging to the pasta—a big drawback. If you sauce the pasta immediately after draining, the noodles won't stick. The only time I add oil to the pasta water is when boiling fresh wide pasta sheets for lasagne or cannelloni. That little slick of oil keeps the cooked sheets from sticking to each other as they wait their turn to go into the baking dish.

Stir the pasta immediately after adding it to the water to keep it from sticking to the bottom of the pot. Stir frequently during the first couple of minutes and occasionally after that.

Don't break long pasta to fit it in the pot. With a few exceptions (see *Spaghetti Spezzati con Piselli*, page 48), long pasta is meant to remain long. Part of the pleasure of eating it is twirling it around your fork, a pleasure diminished if you break the strands.

Unless you have a powerful stove, cover the pot after adding the pasta so the water returns to a boil as quickly as possible. Uncover once the water returns to a boil.

Test pasta for doneness by tasting it. There is no other way. I have cooked so much pasta that I can almost tell when it's done by sight, but I still set a timer and check by taste. Although many pasta packages include recommended cooking times, they are often inaccurate. De Cecco's recommended times are almost uniformly on target, but I distrust most others.

Dried pasta is done when it is no longer hard at the core but still firm and pleasantly chewy. This is what Italians mean by al dente. If it presents no resistance to the tooth, it is overcooked. Fresh pasta should be cooked until it is tender and no longer doughy, but with a slight resistance.

Before you drain the pasta, take out some "insurance." Set aside about 1 cup of the hot pasta water to moisten pasta and sauce after you toss them together. I find that a little additional moisture is almost always needed, especially with fresh pasta.

Drain pasta in a large colander or sieve. Shake a few times to remove excess water, but don't shake it dry. Leave some water clinging to the pasta to help the sauce cloak it nicely. Return it to the warm pot you cooked it in and sauce it immediately.

Never rinse pasta, which would cool it off unnecessarily.

saucing and serving pasta

Use warmed platters and bowls when serving pasta. Either warm them in a low oven or by filling them with hot water until you need them.

Pasta is most appealing when it is lightly sauced so that you can actually taste the noodles. For a clingy sauce, such as one made of tomato or cream, use just enough to coat the noodles. A mere $1^1/_2$ cups of tomato sauce is enough for 1 pound of pasta. There should be no sauce left in the bottom of the bowl when you finish the pasta.

Remember that pasta is bland, so sauces need to be highly seasoned.

For many recipes, I drain the pasta when it is about 1 minute shy of al dente and finish cooking it in the sauce. This technique allows the pasta to absorb some of the flavor of the sauce. It's a good method to use for "saucy" sauces with tomato or cream; when the sauce is predominantly olive oil and vegetables, such as for *Orecchiette con Cime di Rapa e Salsiccia* (page 106), it's less useful.

Cream sauces on fresh pasta are a challenge for novice pasta cooks. If you reduce the cream too much, the pasta will clump. You must keep the sauce much looser than you may imagine because fresh pasta is thirsty and will soak it up. This is especially true if your pasta is freshly made. Drying the pasta for a few hours makes it easier to work with and less absorbent. In any case, when saucing fresh pasta with a cream-based sauce, err on the side of under-reducing it. You can always cook the pasta and sauce together in the skillet if the sauce seems too thin.

You can serve pasta family style from a large platter, or you can serve it already portioned into individual bowls. Although I love the collegiality of serving family style, I usually portion the pasta in the kitchen so that each diner gets the right amount of sauce on the pasta.

about portion size

In my home, 1 pound of pasta serves four people as the main course of a simple dinner. If I'm serving the pasta as a first course or as part of a multicourse meal, I figure 1 pound for six people.

choosing the right shape for your sauce

Italians have firm opinions about which pasta shape goes with which sauce. These ideas aren't whims; they derive from generations of experience and observation. Although some sauces are versatile enough to use on virtually any noodle—short or long, fresh or dried—other sauces and shapes have traditional associations, and with good reason.

With long dried pasta, such as spaghetti or bucatini:
Tomato-based sauces; olive oil–based sauces with chopped vegetables such as broccoli rabe, cauliflower, or radicchio; braised vegetable sauces, such as slow-cooked onions, artichokes, or sweet peppers.

With short dried tubular pasta, such as penne rigate or rigatoni:
Tomato-based sauces; ricotta-based sauces; vegetable purees; baked pastas. Because you can't twirl these shapes, they are difficult to pair with vegetables that are not bound in tomato, béchamel, or cream.

With short dried pasta with hollows, such as fusilli, cavatappi, or conchiglie:
Chunky tomato-based sauces; vegetable purees; braised vegetables; sauces with nuggets of meat or bits of vegetable that can slip into the hollows.

With long fresh pasta, such as fettuccine or pappardelle:
Butter- or cream-based sauces; spring vegetables such as asparagus, artichokes, fava beans, and peas; tomato sauces; mushroom sauces.

With traditional regional shapes such as cavatelli:
Fresh shelling beans or dried beans; tomato sauce

With traditional regional shapes such as orecchiette:
Broccoli rabe; cauliflower; tomato sauce; artichokes; arugula; fava beans

Your pasta-making skills will improve dramatically if you put them to regular use. I discovered this when I moved to a town where I could no longer buy good fresh pasta. If I wanted it, I had to make it myself.

In the years since, I have shaved many minutes off my production time. I can now produce 1 pound of fresh pasta, from start through cleanup, in about 40 minutes. As a result, I no longer think of fresh pasta as a project for weekends only.

Even if you do have a source for high-quality fresh pasta, made daily with whole eggs, I encourage you to try making your own. Once you become comfortable with the motions and the feel of the dough, you will discover that your own pasta far surpasses what you can buy. It is more supple, more flavorful, more delicate. And for some dishes, such as lasagne and ravioli, that call for extra-thin pasta sheets, you may have to make your own. I've never found commercial fresh pasta rolled thin enough for these dishes, and it is often too dry by the time you buy it to roll it thinner at home.

FRESH EGG PASTA

I rarely use extra-large eggs in cooking but I use them in pasta dough. Why? Because when you mix 3 extra-large eggs with enough flour to make a dough, you get about 1 pound of pasta, the required amount for most recipes.

> **Approximately 2½ cups unbleached all-purpose flour**
> **3 extra-large eggs, lightly beaten**

To make the dough: Put the 2^1/$_2$ cups flour on a large work surface. Make a well in the center large enough to contain the eggs. Make sure your flour "walls" are high enough to keep the eggs from escaping. Pour the eggs into the well. With a fork, begin drawing in flour from the sides and whisking it with the eggs. Take care not to let the runny eggs breach the flour walls or you will have a mess. As you incorporate more flour and the egg mixture thickens, you can relax about the walls.

When the dough becomes too stiff to mix with the fork, continue with your hands. You won't be able to incorporate all the flour, at least not at first, but use enough to make a dough you can knead without it sticking to your hands. Sift the remaining flour to remove any coarse particles, and wash your hands to remove any caked-on bits.

Now knead by hand for several minutes, adding as much reserved flour as you need to make a smooth dough without a trace of stickiness. Shape the dough into a rectangle and divide it in half. Set aside one-half, covered with a clean dish towel. Now you will make pasta sheets with the other half, using the pasta machine.

Lightly flour the work surface. Firmly clamp your pasta machine to an immovable surface. Set the rollers on the widest setting. With a rolling pin, flatten the dough into a rectangle thin enough to go through the rollers. Feed it through one time. Lay the resulting ribbon on your lightly floured work surface, then fold it in thirds, matching edges to make a neat rectangle. With the rolling pin, roll it out in the other direction (with the open ends at the top and bottom), flouring as necessary to keep it from sticking. Try to keep the open ends matched up so you continue to have a neat rectangle.

With the roller still on the widest setting, repeat the process at least nine times: feeding the dough through, folding the ribbon in thirds, then flouring and flattening. With each successive trip through the rollers, you should need less flour. At the end of this mechanical kneading, you should have a smooth, silky, well-blended ribbon of dough. If not, continue the process until you do.

To stretch the dough: Now you are ready to begin the stretching process by feeding the ribbon through progressively narrower settings, beginning again with the widest one. Cut the ribbon into manageable lengths whenever it gets too unwieldy. Resist flouring the dough at this point because the flour won't be well incorporated; dust lightly with flour only if the dough threatens to stick to the rollers. I find that setting number 5 on the KitchenAid attachment is thin enough for fettuccine, which should be delicate but not insubstantial. The noodles should be neither so thick that they are chewy, nor so thin that they clump after cooking. Pasta for lasagne and cannelloni should be thinner; I use setting number 6. Pasta for ravioli should be as thin as you can comfortably make it; I use setting number 7. You will need to find the settings you prefer on your own machine, which may take a few attempts. As you finish stretching each sheet, lay it on a clean dish towel to rest.

While you wait for the first batch of sheets to dry, repeat the mechanical kneading and stretching process with the second half of the dough.

To cut the noodles: Depending on how much flour you worked into the dough, the sheets may be ready to cut immediately or they may need to dry awhile. If they feel at all damp, the noodles will stick together when you cut them. Let the sheets air dry, checking them every 30 minutes, until they are no longer damp (but not too dry or they will crack in the cutter).

You can cut the sheets into noodles of the desired width by hand or using the pasta machine's cutting attachments.

To cut the pasta by hand, start at one of the sheet's narrow ends and loosely roll it like a jelly roll, leaving a 1-inch tail. With a sharp chef's knife, cut ribbons of the desired width. Grab the noodles by the exposed ends, lift them up, and they will unfurl.

Arrange the noodles on a dish towel or on a surface lightly dusted with semolina. Let dry at least 30 minutes before cooking.

You can make fresh noodles several hours ahead and keep them at cool room temperature. You can also freeze fresh pasta with some success. Freeze it in a sturdy plastic bag and cook it directly from the freezer; do not thaw first.

FRESH SAFFRON PASTA

You can buy powdered saffron, but I prefer to use saffron threads pounded in a mortar; that way I know I'm getting an unadulterated product.

> Enough saffron threads to yield ⅛ teaspoon powdered saffron
> Approximately 2½ cups unbleached all-purpose flour
> 3 extra-large eggs, lightly beaten

Stir the saffron into the flour, blending well, then proceed according to the directions for Fresh Egg Pasta.

FRESH SPINACH PASTA

> ¾ pound spinach (not baby spinach)
> 2 extra-large eggs
> Approximately 2¾ cups unbleached all-purpose flour

Discard any thick spinach stems. Put the spinach in a large pot with just the wash water clinging to the leaves. Cover and cook over moderate heat until the spinach wilts. Drain and cool under running water, then squeeze to remove as much moisture as possible.

Put the spinach in a food processor with 1 of the eggs. Puree until the spinach is as fine as possible. Beat the other egg in a small bowl.

Put the flour on a large work surface and make a well in the center. Put the spinach and the beaten egg in the well. Proceed according to the directions for Fresh Egg Pasta.

To cut fettuccine or tagliatelle:
Use the wide cutter attachment on the pasta machine to make noodles about $1/4$ inch wide, or cut by hand (page 16) into ribbons $1/4$ to $3/8$ inch wide.

To cut laganelle:
Stretch the pasta sheets as thin as you would for fettuccine. Cut by hand (page 16) into ribbons $1/2$ inch wide.

To cut maltagliati:
In some kitchens, maltagliati, or "badly cut" pasta, are the scraps left over from making another pasta dish, such as ravioli. Mine are a little less random in appearance. To make maltagliati, stretch the pasta sheets as thin as you would for lasagne. Roll each sheet loosely like a jelly roll, leaving a 1-inch tail, then cut by hand into ribbons about $3/4$ inch wide. Unfurl the ribbons, stack them, and cut crosswise, but on an alternating diagonal, to make trapezoids roughly 2 inches in length.

To cut pappardelle:
Stretch the pasta sheets as thin as you would for fettuccine. Keeping the sheets flat, not rolled, cut by hand with a fluted pastry wheel into ribbons $5/8$ inch wide.

To cut tonnarelli:
Tonnarelli are fresh noodles that resemble spaghetti, but they are square in cross section. You can make them with most home pasta machines by not stretching the sheets as thin as you would for fettuccine. (I stop at number 3, two settings before the setting I use for fettuccine.) Then use the narrowest cutter attachment.

To cut trenette:
Stretch the pasta sheets as thin as you would for fettuccine. Cut by hand (page 16) into ribbons slightly narrower than fettuccine, about $3/16$ inch wide.

EQUIPPING THE PASTA KITCHEN

I have eaten exquisite pasta in Italy made in what most Americans would consider a primitive kitchen. You don't need many tools to make good pasta. Nevertheless, a few pieces of kitchen equipment will make the process easier.

Box grater

A four-sided, stainless-steel box grater is useful for grating plum tomatoes into pulp (page 25). I use the large holes for tomatoes and the medium holes for Parmesan and aged pecorino.

Food mill

I occasionally use a food mill to puree canned tomatoes before adding them to a sauce, or to make puree from fresh tomatoes (page 25). Unlike the food processor or blender, the food mill removes the skins and seeds.

Pasta machine

Generations of Italian women have made fresh pasta with nothing more than a work surface and a rolling pin. With such regular upper-arm workouts, they did not need the gym. Nevertheless, we can be grateful for the modern pasta machines that make home production of fresh pasta so easy today.

I have used both the Atlas and Imperia hand-cranked pasta machines and find them good for home use. But if you have a KitchenAid standing mixer, consider purchasing that machine's pasta attachments. They clamp onto the head of the mixer, and the mixer's motor turns the rollers, leaving both of your hands free to feed dough into the rollers. What's more, the heavy mixer stays securely in place; it doesn't "walk" like the hand-cranked machines tend to do, no matter how firmly you clamp them. I think the KitchenAid attachments are a great leap forward in home pasta production.

I have never used the kind of pasta machine that mixes and kneads the dough for you. For me, a great part of the pleasure of making pasta is getting my hands in the flour and egg and feeling the pasta dough take shape.

Pastry wheel

Many pastry wheels actually have two wheels attached to one handle. One wheel has a straight edge, the other a fluted edge. I use the straight-edged wheel to cut some pasta shapes by hand, such as the semolina noodles for *Pasta e Ceci* (page 116). I use the fluted cutter to give a rippled edge to some pasta shapes, such as ravioli (page 87).

Wire-mesh skimmer

You will need a flat skimmer or strainer to lift ravioli out of the boiling pasta water. They are too delicate to drain in a sieve.

ABOUT INGREDIENTS

Good ingredients are the foundation of all good cooking. Whether you are purchasing preserved anchovies, canned tomatoes, or olive oil for your pasta pantry, select for quality, not price. On a cost-per-serving basis, the difference between a good brand and an inferior brand will be insignificant, but it can make a big difference to your results.

Anchovies

I suspect that so many people dislike anchovies because they have never tasted good ones. If I could, I would serve all these reluctant anchovy eaters the meaty, mild Sicilian anchovies packed by Agostino Recca, available today in many markets. These superior preserved fish are tasty enough to eat on their own, with a little minced garlic, chopped parsley, extra-virgin olive oil, and good bread.

Many canneries use strong jets of water to clean anchovies during processing, which beats up the delicate fish. At Recca, the fish are cleaned carefully by hand to preserve their integrity.

Recca packs anchovies both whole in salt and filleted in olive oil. I prefer the fillets because they come in small jars that you can use up quickly, before the fish oils oxidize. If you don't use all the anchovies, top off the jar with extra-virgin olive oil and refrigerate it. The olive oil protects the fish oils from oxidizing, but not indefinitely; try to finish the jar within a week or two.

Many professional chefs prefer Recca's whole, salt-packed anchovies, but they come in large tins and the anchovies go rancid before I get to the bottom. They must be rinsed of their salt and filleted before using. If you open the whole tin and don't expect to go through it immediately, it's a good idea to rinse and fillet all the anchovies and repack them in olive oil to cover, then refrigerate.

I never buy the salt-packed anchovies that some markets sell by weight from open tins. Unless the tin was freshly opened, the anchovies will likely be faintly or even flagrantly rancid.

Bread Crumbs

In southern Italy, especially in Sicily, some pasta preparations are finished with a sprinkling of toasted bread crumbs instead of cheese. Probably this practice dates from bleaker times, when many households had no money for cheese but were never without stale bread.

Even today, frugal Italian cooks always have homemade bread crumbs around. When toasted, the crumbs add an appealing crunch and substance to some pasta dishes, such as *Spaghetti con Radicchio alla Piemontese* (page 90). The bread crumbs replace cheese; they are never used with it.

Bread crumbs for pasta should be almost as fine as cracker crumbs. To make them, use a country-style bread that contains only flour, water, yeast, and salt. Don't use breads that have fat or sugar in them. The bread should be quite stale. If it isn't, dry it out in a low oven. Let cool, then break into chunks, crust and all, and put the chunks in a food processor. Process until the crumbs are fine. If the crumbs remain coarse, the bread is probably not dry enough. Spread the crumbs on a baking sheet and put them back in the low oven until they dry further, then cool and process again.

Sieve the crumbs to remove the coarsest ones. If you have enough coarse crumbs, you can process and sieve them one more time. Discard any crumbs that fail to go through the sieve the second time. Half a pound of stale bread should yield about 1 cup of fine crumbs.

Store bread crumbs in an airtight container in the freezer. They will keep for 6 months.

To toast bread crumbs: Heat 1 tablespoon extra-virgin olive oil in a small skillet over moderately low heat. Add 1/2 cup fine bread crumbs and stir to coat with the oil. Season lightly with salt. Cook, stirring often, over moderately low heat until the crumbs are an even, deep golden brown, about 10 minutes. Set aside to cool.

Cheese

Cheese is an indispensable addition to many vegetable sauces for pasta, but it is often overused and sometimes unnecessary. Don't reach for the Parmesan reflexively; instead, think about whether cheese would enhance the dish you are making. In some cases, cheese would mask the fresh, pure taste of the vegetables or make a simple dish overly rich. When I do put cheese on vegetable-sauced pasta, I tend to use it sparingly.

For saucing pasta with vegetables, the most useful cheeses are Parmigiano-Reggiano; an aged pecorino such as pecorino romano or pecorino sardo; and ricotta salata.

Parmigiano-Reggiano: This is one cheese I am never without. Look for the name stamped on the rind to be sure you are getting authentic Parmigiano-Reggiano from Italy, not the younger and less flavorful Grana Padano or the unsatisfying American and Argentinian versions of Parmesan. Parmigiano-Reggiano has a deep, complex, well-balanced flavor that its imitators don't begin to match.

Always buy Parmigiano-Reggiano in chunks and grate it as you need it. Pregrated Parmesan quickly loses its savor. At the store, look for wedges with as little rind as possible to get the most cheese for your dollar. If the cheese is plastic wrapped, take it out of the plastic at home and rewrap it in aluminum foil, then refrigerate. It will keep for weeks. Change the foil wrap every time you use the cheese.

Pecorino: In Italian, the name *pecorino* signifies that the cheese is made from sheep's milk. (*Pecora* is Italian for sheep.) Italy produces dozens of pecorino cheeses of various styles. Some are young, mild, and creamy; others are well-aged and rock-hard, with the sharp, salty flavor that most Americans associate with pecorino.

Aged pecorino is a superb grating cheese for many vegetable-sauced pastas, often surpassing Parmesan to my taste. It complements sauces made with tomato, cauliflower, broccoli, broccoli rabe, eggplant, green beans, or fava beans. Sauces of southern Italian origin—as so many vegetable sauces are—tend to call for pecorino over Parmesan, a cheese of the north.

The most widely available aged pecorinos in this country are pecorino romano and pecorino sardo, with romano the more common. Both are grating cheeses, and either type will work in these recipes. As with Parmesan, pecorino is best grated as you need it. It keeps for weeks, so don't hesitate to buy a large chunk. Store it in the refrigerator, wrapped in aluminum foil, and change the wrap whenever you use the cheese.

Ricotta salata: When salted, pressed, and matured for a few weeks, fresh ricotta is transformed into a firm, dense, chalk-white cheese that you can grate or shave with a cheese plane into fine shards. It has a mild saltiness and recognizable sheep's-milk character. I don't find it particularly appealing as a table cheese, but it is a wonderful complement to many vegetable-sauced pastas. I particularly like it with sauces that include tomato, eggplant, fava beans, green beans, or broccoli.

Despite its dry appearance, ricotta salata is not a great keeper once cut. I try to use it within a few days of purchase, before it develops a sourish smell and taste. Keep it wrapped in aluminum foil in the refrigerator.

Chiles

Calabrian chiles: From Italy's Calabria region, these small red chiles packed in olive oil have a fruity dimension in addition to their heat. I like to use them in sauces that aren't cooked, such as *Penne "Orchidee delle Eolie"* (page 67). When making cooked sauces, I tend to reach for hot pepper flakes out of habit, but these flavorful chiles would be excellent for that use, too.

Hot pepper flakes: I count on hot pepper flakes to add an undercurrent of warmth to many pasta sauces. You can make them yourself by pulverizing small dried red chiles in a spice grinder, or you can buy them already ground on most supermarket spice racks.

Because brands vary in their pungency, I'm reluctant to specify a quantity of hot pepper flakes in recipes. Instead, I have called for a pinch, which you can adjust up or down to your taste. To my palate, 1/4 teaspoon of hot pepper flakes is about right for sauces that cover 1 pound of pasta.

Keep hot pepper flakes in a cool, dark, dry place as you would other spices. They will stay potent for at least 1 year.

Nuts

Pine nuts, almonds, and walnuts enhance many vegetable sauces, adding richness and texture. In some recipes, such as *Trenette al Pesto* (page 56) or *Spaghetti ai Capperi* (page 68), they act as a thickener. I always toast nuts before using to heighten their flavor.

To toast nuts: Preheat the oven to 325° or 350°F. Put the nuts on a rimmed baking sheet or, if the amount is small, in a metal pie tin. Bake until the nuts are fragrant and lightly colored, shaking the pan once or twice. Pine nuts take 5 to 10 minutes, almonds and walnuts a little longer. With almonds and walnuts, break one open to make sure it's toasty throughout. Let cool before using to allow them to crisp.

Porcini Mushrooms

Many supermarkets now carry dried porcini (*Boletus edulis*) in plastic packages, and many delis sell them by the ounce, which is usually a better buy. These dried mushrooms must be reconstituted before using. Put them in a small bowl and add enough lukewarm water that they swim a bit. (Most recipes call for using some or all of the soaking liquid, so don't dilute its flavor by using more water than necessary.) Let the mushrooms stand until softened, 30 minutes to 1 hour. Lift them out of the soaking liquid with a slotted spoon to leave any grit behind. Strain the liquid through a damp paper towel or a double thickness of cheesecloth, also damp (to prevent the straining medium from soaking up the flavorful liquid), and use as called for in the recipe.

Keep dried porcini in an airtight container in a cool place. They will keep indefinitely.

Salt

I use only sea salt or kosher salt for seasoning pasta sauces and encourage you to do the same. Iodized table salt such as Morton's contains dextrose and an anti-caking additive that give the salt a harsh taste. In contrast, many sea salts and all true kosher salts have no additives. I prefer the flavor of sea salt, but kosher salt is a good alternative.

Tomatoes

Fresh tomatoes: In summer and fall, I use fresh tomatoes for pasta sauce—almost exclusively the meaty plum tomatoes. These tomatoes, also known as Roma or paste tomatoes, have a high proportion of flesh to juice, so you don't have to cook them long to get a thick, tasty sauce. Slicing or salad tomatoes have higher water content and are not well suited to cooked sauces. I use them in summery raw sauces where their flavor really shines, such as *Spaghetti con Salsa Rapida* (page 71).

In times past, I would peel, seed, and dice fresh plum tomatoes for sauce. Then I learned an easier way. Grating plum tomatoes produces a skinless, seedless pulp in less time, with less equipment. To grate tomatoes, you need a four-sided, stainless-steel box grater. Cut the tomatoes in half and scoop out the seeds and juice with your fingers. Holding the cut side of a tomato half against the grater's large holes, grate until only the thin tomato skin remains in your palm.

Sometimes I want a smoother tomato texture than the box grater yields. To make pureed fresh plum tomatoes, cut them in half lengthwise, then pass them through the medium blade of a food mill to remove the skins and seeds.

A handful of my recipes call for peeled, seeded, and diced tomato, not pulp. Here's how to do that:

Bring a pot of water to a boil over high heat. Have ready a bowl of ice water. Cut an X in the rounded end of each tomato. Place them in the boiling water and simmer about 30 seconds. (Less ripe tomatoes may need a little longer.) Transfer them with a slotted spoon to the ice water to stop the cooking. When cool, lift the tomatoes out of the ice water and peel them; the skin should peel back easily from the X. Core, cut in half, and scoop out the seeds and juice with your fingers. Then chop as the recipe specifies.

Canned tomatoes: Canned tomatoes are not a second-best substitute for fresh tomatoes. In winter and spring, when fresh plum tomatoes are rock-hard, slippery with wax, and tasteless, canned tomatoes are by far the better choice for sauces.

However, there are canned tomatoes and canned tomatoes. Because they are critical to the flavor of your sauces, take some time to compare the brands available to you. Seek out the packers that consistently use ripe, meaty tomatoes and pack them in flavorful, not watery, juice. It is not true that imported brands are always better.

When using canned tomatoes, you can chop them finely first or simply crush them between your fingers as you add them to the skillet.

The baking soda trick: Unless you are using sweet, height-of-summer tomatoes, chances are your tomato sauce will taste more tart than you might like. Many recipes call for adding a pinch of sugar in that case, but sugar doesn't eliminate the tartness; it just makes the sauce sweeter. Nevertheless, I did that for years until my scientist husband reminded me that the way to neutralize an acid is with a base. He suggested adding a pinch of baking soda to overly tart tomato sauce.

It works like a charm. You don't need much baking soda to have an impact, so start with a pinch. The sauce will foam briefly as you stir it in. Let the sauce simmer for a minute or so, then taste again. Add a little more baking soda if necessary. Be careful not to add too much or your sauce will taste soapy.

I almost always use baking soda when making a sauce with canned tomatoes, and even sometimes when fresh tomatoes yield a sauce that needs mellowing.

After months of eating winter's rugged vegetables, preparing pasta with spring produce feels like throwing off a heavy cloak. By mid-February I am craving asparagus, but I try not to leap on the first shipments, knowing that tastier spears will soon follow the pale ones the growers rush to market.

Next, usually by mid-March, come the artichokes from coastal California—baby chokes the size of eggs to braise and toss with orecchiette and bread crumbs, and jumbo specimens with meaty bottoms to sauce maltagliati.

By mid-April, my own garden is yielding the first velvety fava beans. Simmered briefly with a mint sprig and a touch of garlic, they make a simple pasta sauce. A little later, as the beans grow fleshier and firmer, I'll make Sicilian *maccu*, long-braised favas with fennel, to serve with fusilli.

Peas bring up the rear, as spring segues into summer, and for a brief few weeks there's the possibility of *frittella*—the Sicilian spring vegetable stew. Tossed with fresh or dried pasta, it's a highlight of the season.

spring recipes

EAR-SHAPED PASTA WITH BABY ARTICHOKES, WHITE WINE, GARLIC, PARSLEY, AND BREAD CRUMBS

In fertile Puglia, the "heel" of Italy's boot, no scrap of land lies bare if it can possibly nourish an artichoke plant or a few tomatoes. Farmers even grow cauliflower, broccoli rabe, and other vegetables between the neat rows of their olive trees, apparently determined to squeeze the highest return from what ground they have. A good share of the harvest ends up in the family pasta pot, paired with the signature shape of the region: orecchiette. The vegetables, like the artichokes in this recipe, are always fully cooked, never al dente, to produce a simple but deeply flavorful sauce for the sturdy pasta. **Serves 4 to 6**

1 lemon

24 baby artichokes, 1½ to 2 ounces each

8 tablespoons extra-virgin olive oil

Salt and a pinch of hot pepper flakes

¼ cup dry white wine

4 cloves garlic, minced

¼ cup minced fresh Italian (flat-leaf) parsley

1 pound orecchiette

¼ cup toasted bread crumbs (page 22), plus more for passing at the table

Fill a large bowl with water and add the juice of the lemon. To trim the artichokes, peel back the outer leaves until they break off at the base. Keep removing leaves until you reach the pale green heart. Cut across the top of the heart to remove the pointed leaf tips. If the stem is still attached, cut it down to 1/2 inch, then trim the stem and base to remove any dark green or brown parts. Cut each heart into 6 or 8 wedges, then immediately place in the lemon water to prevent browning.

Heat 6 tablespoons of the olive oil in a large skillet over moderate heat. Drain the artichokes and add them to the skillet. Season with salt to taste and the hot pepper flakes. Add the wine and 1/4 cup water. Bring the liquid to a simmer, then cover, adjust the heat to maintain a gentle simmer, and cook until the artichokes are very tender and beginning to break apart, 30 to 35 minutes. Uncover occasionally, stir, and add more water if the mixture threatens to cook dry.

While the artichokes are cooking, bring a large pot of salted water to a boil. When the artichokes are tender, stir in the garlic and parsley. Cook for a couple of minutes to release their flavor. Keep the artichokes warm over low heat.

Add the pasta to the boiling water and cook until al dente. Drain the pasta and return it to the warm pot over low heat. Add the remaining 2 tablespoons olive oil and toss well, then add the artichokes. Toss again, divide the pasta among warm bowls, and sprinkle each portion with some of the bread crumbs. Pass the additional bread crumbs at the table.

"BADLY CUT PASTA" WITH ARTICHOKES AND AIR-DRIED BEEF

In the Sicilian countryside near Ragusa, my husband, Doug, and I stayed at a former monastery that had been converted into a comfortable small inn. The handsome restaurant at the Eremo della Giubiliana drew from its own garden for some of its dishes, including this one.

Although you must remove the artichoke leaves and use only the bottoms, don't throw away the leaves. Steam them the next day and enjoy them with a vinaigrette or aioli for dipping.

Look for speck at specialty-food stores. Prosciutto can be substituted. **Serves 4 to 6**

1 lemon

4 large artichokes

6 tablespoons extra-virgin olive oil, plus more for drizzling

1 yellow onion, minced

Pinch of hot pepper flakes

1 bay leaf

Salt

2 tablespoons chopped fresh Italian (flat-leaf) parsley

2 ounces speck (air-dried beef) or prosciutto, thinly sliced, then julienned

3/4 pound Fresh Egg Pasta (page 14), cut as maltagliati (page 18)

Fill a large bowl with water and add the juice of the lemon. To trim the artichokes, peel back the tough outer leaves until they break off at the base. Keep removing leaves until you reach the pale yellow-green heart. Cut across the heart, leaving only about 3/4 inch of leaf attached to the base. Cut off all but 1 inch of the stem, if attached, then trim the stem and base to remove any dark green or brown parts. Cut the trimmed artichoke in half. With a spoon, scoop out the fuzzy choke and the prickly inner leaves. Cut each half into thin wedges and immediately place them in the lemon water to prevent browning.

Heat the olive oil in a large skillet over moderately low heat. Add the onion and hot pepper flakes and sauté until the onion is soft, about 10 minutes. Drain the artichokes and add them to the skillet. Add the bay leaf, 1 cup water, and a generous pinch of salt. Bring to a simmer, cover, and adjust the heat to maintain a gentle simmer. Cook, stirring occasionally, until the artichokes are tender, 15 to 20 minutes. There should be a few tablespoons of flavorful juices left in the skillet. (If the artichokes threaten to cook dry before they are tender, add a little water.) Remove the bay leaf and gently stir in the parsley and speck.

While the artichokes are cooking, bring a large pot of salted water to a boil over high heat. Add the pasta and cook until about 1 minute shy of al dente. Set aside 1 cup of the pasta water, then drain the pasta and return it to the warm pot over low heat. Add the sauce and cook for about 1 minute to allow the pasta to absorb some of the flavor of the sauce. Moisten with some of the reserved pasta water as needed. Divide among warm bowls and drizzle each portion with a little olive oil. Serve immediately.

Bucatini con Carciofi alla Pugliese

LONG PIERCED PASTA WITH ARTICHOKES, PANCETTA, EGGS, AND PECORINO

Like the familiar spaghetti carbonara, this artichoke sauce depends on eggs to make it thick and creamy. The beaten eggs must be added off the heat or they will scramble; you don't want to see any trace of cooked egg or egg white. Because the technique is a little challenging, you may want to have a practice run before you make this dish for guests.

I have found similar recipes for artichoke sauces in several cookbooks from Puglia. This version is based on one in *The Land of Olive Trees*, edited by Mario Adda. **Serves 4 to 6**

1 lemon

4 large artichokes

⅓ cup extra-virgin olive oil

3 ounces pancetta, minced

1 large yellow onion, minced

Salt and freshly ground black pepper

¾ cup dry white wine

1 pound bucatini (perciatelli) or spaghetti

2 eggs, lightly beaten

⅔ cup freshly grated aged pecorino cheese

Fill a large bowl with water and add the juice of the lemon. To trim the artichokes, peel back the tough outer leaves until they break off at the base. Keep removing leaves until you reach the pale yellow-green heart. (You can steam the leaves the following day, if desired, and enjoy them with a dipping sauce.) Cut across the heart, leaving only about 3/4 inch of leaf attached to the base. Cut off all but 1 inch of the stem, if attached, then trim the stem and base to remove any dark green or brown parts. Cut the trimmed artichoke in half. With a spoon, scoop out the fuzzy choke and the prickly inner leaves. Cut each half into thin wedges and immediately place them in the lemon water to prevent browning.

Put the olive oil, pancetta, and onion in a cold skillet and cook over moderately low heat, stirring, until the onion is soft, 10 to 12 minutes. Drain the artichokes and add them to the skillet. Season with salt to taste and add the wine. Stir gently and simmer uncovered for 3 to 4 minutes to allow the alcohol to evaporate, then add 3/4 cup water, cover, and continue cooking until the artichokes are tender, 30 minutes or longer. There should still be a little liquid left in the skillet. (If the artichokes threaten to cook dry before they are tender, add a little water.) Taste and adjust the salt, then set the sauce aside to cool for at least 10 minutes.

Bring a large pot of salted water to a boil over high heat. Add the pasta and cook until al dente.

About 2 minutes before the pasta is done, stir the eggs into the cooled sauce, then return the sauce to low heat. Cook gently, stirring constantly, until the sauce just begins to thicken; if you cook it too quickly, the eggs will curdle.

Drain the pasta and return it to the warm pot over low heat. Add the sauce and toss well. The heat of the noodles will thicken the sauce further and make it creamy. Add the cheese and several grindings of black pepper and toss again. Serve in warm bowls.

Pasta con la Frittella

FRESH PASTA WITH BRAISED ARTICHOKES, FAVA BEANS, AND PEAS

Visiting Sicily in late April, at the height of the season for artichokes and fava beans, my husband, Doug, and I encountered *frittella* at every turn. A spring stew of artichokes, fava beans, and peas, it appears on restaurant and family tables as a first course, a light lunch dish, or a *contorno* (side dish). We often had it over pasta, both fresh and dried. It keeps well for a day or two, so you might want to double the sauce and enjoy half of it over pasta one day and the other half for lunch with bread the next.

Frittella, also called *frittedda*, is typically cooked well beyond al dente, until the flavors merge and deepen. Don't expect a spring-green appearance. **Serves 4 to 6**

1 lemon

16 to 20 baby artichokes, about 1½ ounces each

8 tablespoons extra-virgin olive oil

1 small yellow onion, minced

4 cloves garlic, coarsely chopped

Pinch of hot pepper flakes

Salt

2 pounds fresh fava beans, shelled but not peeled

1 pound English peas, shelled (about 1 cup)

¼ cup chopped fresh basil

1 pound Fresh Egg Pasta (page 14), cut as fettuccine (page 18), or dried orecchiette or tubetti

Fill a large bowl with water and add the juice of the lemon. To trim the artichokes, peel back the outer leaves until they break off at the base. Keep removing leaves until you reach the pale green heart. Cut across the top of the heart to remove the pointed leaf tips. If the stem is still attached, cut it down to $1/2$ inch, then trim the stem and base to remove any dark green or brown parts. Cut each heart into 6 or 8 wedges, then immediately place in the lemon water to prevent browning.

Heat 6 tablespoons of the olive oil in a large skillet over moderately low heat. Add the onion, garlic, and hot pepper flakes and cook until the onion is soft, about 10 minutes. Drain the artichokes and add them to the skillet. Season with salt to taste and add 1 cup water. Cover and adjust the heat to maintain a gentle simmer. Cook 10 minutes, then add the fava beans, peas, and 1 cup additional water. Cover and simmer until the vegetables are tender, about 15 minutes longer. Stir in the basil and cook for another minute or two. At the end of the cooking time, the liquid should have reduced to a few tablespoons of flavorful pan juices. If not, uncover and simmer until reduced. Taste and adjust the seasoning.

Bring a large pot of salted water to a boil over high heat. Add the pasta and cook until about 1 minute shy of al dente. Set aside 1 cup of the pasta water, then drain the pasta and return it to the warm pot over moderately low heat. Add the sauce and the remaining 2 tablespoons olive oil and cook for about 1 minute to allow the pasta to absorb some of the flavor of the sauce. Moisten with some of the reserved pasta water as needed. Divide among warm bowls and serve immediately.

SPAGHETTI WITH ASPARAGUS, FRIED EGGS, BLACK PEPPER, AND PECORINO

I've always loved asparagus with fried eggs on top, the eggs cooked briskly so the whites get crisp but the yolks stay runny. Tossed with pasta, it's a one-dish meal. Timing is critical—you want the eggs, asparagus, and pasta done at the same time—so I never attempt the dish for more than two. **Serves 2**

1 pound asparagus

4 tablespoons extra-virgin olive oil

Salt and freshly ground black pepper

½ pound spaghetti

2 eggs

3 tablespoons freshly grated aged pecorino cheese or toasted bread crumbs (page 22), plus more for topping

Preheat the oven to 425°F. Bring a large pot of salted water to a boil over high heat.

Holding an asparagus spear in both hands, bend the spear gently. It will break naturally at the point at which the spear becomes tough. Repeat with the remaining asparagus. Discard the tough ends. Cut the trimmed spears on the diagonal into ¹/₂-inch pieces, leaving the tips whole. Put the asparagus in a baking dish or on a baking sheet big enough to hold them in a single layer. Toss with 2 tablespoons of the olive oil and season with salt and pepper to taste. Bake until sizzling and tender, about 15 minutes.

While the asparagus is baking, add the pasta to the boiling water and cook until al dente. About 2 minutes before the pasta is done, heat a skillet over moderately high heat. Add the remaining 2 tablespoons olive oil. When the oil is hot, break in the eggs, season with salt and pepper to taste, and cook, without turning, just until the whites are barely firm. The yolks should remain runny.

Drain the pasta and return it to the warm pot. Add the asparagus and any oil in the baking dish, then add the eggs and any oil in the skillet. Toss well, breaking up the eggs as you toss. The runny yolks will coat the spaghetti with a creamy sauce. Add the cheese or bread crumbs, then add a few grindings of black pepper. Toss again and serve immediately in warm bowls, topping with additional cheese or bread crumbs.

Laganelle allo Zafferano con Punte di Asparagi "Hotel Montinope"

FRESH SAFFRON PASTA WITH ASPARAGUS, LEMON, AND CREAM

While visiting the small factory in Italy's Abruzzo region where Rustichella pasta is produced, I stayed at the comfortable Hotel Montinope in Spoltore. I rarely have high expectations for hotel food, but the chef produced this memorable pasta dish for lunch one day. The saffron turned the noodles a rich golden yellow, as if they had been made with duck eggs. You could taste the saffron, too, and it struck me as just the right complement for a sauce of asparagus, lemon, and cream. No cheese on this pasta, please. **Serves 4 to 6**

1 pound Fresh Saffron Pasta (page 17), cut as laganelle (page 18)

1½ pounds asparagus

1 cup heavy cream

½ cup homemade chicken stock or canned low-sodium broth

3 tablespoons unsalted butter

2 tablespoons thinly sliced chives

¾ teaspoon grated lemon zest

Salt and freshly ground black pepper

Lay the fresh pasta ribbons on clean dish towels and let dry for several hours.

Bring a large pot of salted water to a boil over high heat.

Holding an asparagus spear in both hands, bend the spear gently. It will break naturally at the point at which the spear becomes tough. Repeat with the remaining asparagus. Discard the tough ends. Cut the trimmed spears on the diagonal into 1-inch pieces. Add the asparagus to the boiling water. (I put the pieces in a sieve that fits inside the pot, resting on the edges, so I can lift them out easily.)

While the asparagus is cooking, put the cream, stock, and butter in a large skillet and bring to a simmer over moderate heat. Simmer briefly to thicken slightly. Do not over-reduce, as the pasta will absorb a lot of sauce.

When the asparagus pieces are just tender, 4 to 5 minutes, lift them out of the boiling water with a sieve or skimmer and transfer them to the cream sauce. Keep the cooking water at a boil. Stir the chives and lemon zest into the sauce and season with salt and pepper to taste.

Add the pasta to the boiling water and cook until just shy of al dente. Set aside 1 cup of the pasta water, then drain the pasta and return it to the warm pot over moderately low heat. Add the sauce and cook until the pasta absorbs most of it, moistening with some of the reserved pasta water as needed. The dish should be creamy, not soupy. Divide among warm bowls and serve immediately.

HAND-CUT WIDE NOODLES WITH ASPARAGUS, BUTTER, AND CHEESE

My favorite asparagus sauces for pasta preserve the vegetable's fresh spring taste. With asparagus, less is definitely more. Here I boil the sliced spears briskly to retain their bright color, then toss them with fresh noodles, sweet butter, a little cheese, a scattering of parsley, good sea salt, and black pepper from a mill. Nothing else could improve it. **Serves 6**

1½ pounds asparagus

8 tablespoons unsalted butter, in 8 pieces

1 pound Fresh Egg Pasta (page 14), cut as pappardelle or maltagliati (page 18)

3 tablespoons chopped fresh Italian (flat-leaf) parsley

½ cup freshly grated Parmesan cheese

Salt and freshly ground black pepper

Bring a large pot of salted water to a boil over high heat. Put a serving bowl in a low oven to warm.

Holding an asparagus spear in both hands, bend the spear gently. It will break naturally at the point at which the spear becomes tough. Repeat with the remaining asparagus. Discard the tough ends. Cut the trimmed spears on the diagonal into $^{1}/_{2}$-inch pieces, leaving the tips whole.

Add the asparagus to the boiling water and cook until tender, about 5 minutes. (I put the pieces in a sieve that fits inside the pot, resting on the edges, so I can lift them out easily.) Transfer the asparagus with a sieve or skimmer to the warm bowl. Keep the cooking water at a boil. Put the butter pieces on top of the asparagus and return the bowl to the oven.

Add the pasta to the boiling water and cook until al dente. Set aside 1 cup of the pasta water, then drain the pasta and add it to the bowl with the asparagus. Add the parsley and toss until the butter melts. Add the cheese and salt and pepper to taste. Toss again, moistening with some of the reserved pasta water as needed. Serve immediately in warm bowls.

Penne con Salsa di Asparagi

PENNE WITH CREAMY SICILIAN ASPARAGUS SAUCE

One night in Palermo, my husband, Doug, and I were enjoying the *passeggiata*, the evening stroll, on the grand Viale della Libertà when we passed by a sidewalk book vendor selling inexpensive paperbacks. For the equivalent of three dollars, I purchased *La Pasta Siciliana* by Mariella Conti, a skimpy, low-budget book that proved to be full of interesting recipes, albeit with sketchy directions. I was intrigued by this asparagus sauce, which I have adapted to my taste. With its butter and cream, it hardly seems Sicilian, but it is delicious. **Serves 4 to 6**

4 eggs

1½ pounds asparagus

4 tablespoons unsalted butter, at room temperature

¼ cup heavy cream

Salt and freshly ground black pepper

1 pound penne rigate or other short dried pasta

Freshly grated Parmesan cheese

Put the eggs in a saucepan and cover with cold water. Bring to a boil over high heat, then cover and remove from the heat. Let stand for 8 minutes. Drain and cool under cold running water. Peel the eggs, halve them, and set aside the yolks. (You can eat the whites, sprinkled with salt and pepper, or reserve them for stuffing the next day with tuna salad.)

Holding an asparagus spear in both hands, bend the spear gently. It will break naturally at the point at which the spear becomes tough. Repeat with the remaining asparagus. Discard the tough ends.

Bring a large pot of salted water to a boil over high heat. Add the asparagus and cook until tender, about 5 minutes. Lift the spears out with tongs and cool quickly under cold running water. Keep the cooking water at a boil. Pat the asparagus dry. Line the spears up and cut crosswise into 4 or 5 pieces each. Put the asparagus, cooked egg yolks, and butter in a food processor and puree until smooth.

Transfer the mixture to a skillet and add the cream. Reheat gently, stirring to incorporate the cream. Season well with salt and pepper.

Add the pasta to the boiling water and cook until al dente. Set aside 1 cup of the pasta water, then drain the pasta and return it to the warm pot over low heat. Add enough of the sauce to coat the pasta nicely, moistening with some of the reserved pasta water as needed. You may have some extra sauce.

Divide the pasta among warm bowls, sprinkle a little cheese over each portion, and serve immediately.

SPAGHETTI WITH FAVA BEANS, MINT, AND RICOTTA SALATA

. . . .

A sprig or two of fresh mint in the pot gives braised fava beans a bright, herbal flavor. After tossing the sauce with pasta, I grate in a generous amount of ricotta salata, a young, chalk-white sheep's milk cheese, to provide a faintly salty complement for the sweet favas.

For this dish, it's worth it to spend a little extra on a high-end pasta brand, such as Rustichella, Martelli, or Latini. The rough texture of these brands is a pleasing contrast to the silky fava beans, and it gives the beans something to cling to. **Serves 4 to 6**

. . . .

4 pounds fresh fava beans

6 tablespoons extra-virgin olive oil

1 small yellow onion, minced

2 cloves garlic, smashed

Pinch of hot pepper flakes

Two 4-inch sprigs fresh mint

Salt

1 pound spaghetti

3 to 4 ounces ricotta salata cheese

Have ready a bowl of ice water. Shell the fava beans. Bring a large pot of water to a boil over high heat. Add the shelled beans and blanch for 30 seconds to 1 minute, depending on their size, then drain and transfer them to the ice water. When cool, drain again. Peel the beans; the skins should slip off easily. You should have $1\frac{1}{2}$ to 2 cups.

Heat the olive oil in a large skillet over moderately low heat. Add the onion, garlic, hot pepper flakes, and mint sprigs and cook until the onion is soft, about 10 minutes. Add the fava beans, a generous pinch of salt, and enough water to cover the beans completely ($1\frac{1}{2}$ to 2 cups). Bring to a simmer, cover partially, and simmer gently until the beans are tender, about 15 minutes. The liquid should be nicely flavored and somewhat reduced but still brothy. Add a little water as the beans cook as needed. Remove the garlic and the mint sprigs.

Bring a large pot of salted water to a boil over high heat. Add the pasta and cook until about 1 minute shy of al dente. Set aside 1 cup of the pasta water, then drain the pasta and return it to the warm pot over moderately low heat. Add the sauce and cook for about 1 minute to allow the pasta to absorb some of the flavor of the sauce. Moisten with some of the reserved pasta water as needed.

Grate the cheese into the pasta and toss again, then divide the pasta among warm bowls and serve immediately.

Pizzichi con le Fave alla Nicolina

NICOLINA'S FARRO PASTA WITH FAVA BEANS AND GARLIC CHILE OIL

Nicolina Peduzzi is the matriarch of the family that owns Rustichella pasta, a premium brand from the Abruzzo. A petite and stylish woman who cooks lunch and dinner for eight to ten people every day— her married children and their children come home for lunch—she is a naturally confident cook.

In contrast to Americans who think they have to have all the latest cooking gear, Nicolina works in a modest kitchen and doesn't appear to own a cutting board or a chef's knife. She does all her slicing and chopping with a dull table knife, directly over the pot. With this fava bean sauce, she pairs a farro pasta (farro is a wheat relative) called *pizzichi* (see Resources, page 123), a short, broad shape roughly 1 1/2 inches long. Whole-wheat linguine are more widely available and an appropriate substitute.

Fava bean pods look something like overgrown Kentucky Wonder beans. They are long, flat, and thick-skinned, with the beans nestled inside in a velvety bed. After removing the beans from the pod, an easy task, you still need to peel the more stubborn skins from the beans for most recipes, including this one. These thin skins are slightly bitter.

Nicolina does not approve of my method of blanching the fava beans first to make them easier to peel. She shells and peels them without blanching, claiming that blanching removes flavor and nutrients. That's a price I'm willing to pay for convenience. **Serves 4 to 6**

4 pounds fresh fava beans

1/4 cup extra-virgin olive oil

1/2 yellow onion, minced

2 bay leaves

2 cloves garlic, smashed

Pinch of hot pepper flakes

Salt

1 pound farro pizzichi (see Resources, page 123), farro spaghetti, whole-wheat linguine, or 1 pound Fresh Egg Pasta (page 14), cut as maltagliati (page 18)

Have ready a bowl of ice water. Shell the fava beans. Bring a large pot of water to a boil over high heat. Add the shelled beans and blanch for 30 seconds to 1 minute, depending on their size, then drain and transfer them to the ice water. When cool, drain again. Peel the beans; the skins should slip off easily. You should have 1 1/2 to 2 cups.

Heat the olive oil in a skillet over moderately low heat. Add the onion, bay leaves, smashed garlic, and hot pepper flakes and cook until the onion is soft, about 10 minutes. Add the fava beans, a generous pinch of salt, and 1 cup water. Bring to a simmer, cover partially, and adjust the heat to maintain a gentle simmer. Cook until the fava beans are tender, about 20 minutes. Add more water as needed to keep the beans moist and brothy. When the beans are tender, remove the bay leaves and garlic. Taste and adjust the seasoning. The beans must be well salted or the pasta will taste flat.

(continued)

NICOLINA'S FARRO PASTA WITH FAVA BEANS AND GARLIC CHILE OIL (CONTINUED)

For the Garlic Chile Oil:

¼ cup extra-virgin olive oil

3 cloves garlic, coarsely chopped

3 tablespoons coarsely chopped dried sweet chiles, such as New Mexico chiles

While the beans are cooking, bring a large pot of salted water to a boil over high heat. Add the pasta to the boiling water.

While the pasta is cooking, make the Garlic Chile Oil: Combine the olive oil, chopped garlic, and chiles in a small skillet over moderate heat and cook until the garlic is golden and both the garlic and chiles become crisp. Do not let them burn. Set aside.

When the pasta is about 1 minute shy of al dente, set aside 1 cup of the pasta water, then drain. Return the pasta to the warm pot over moderately low heat and add the fava beans. Cook for about 1 minute to allow the pasta to absorb some of the flavor of the sauce. Moisten with some of the reserved pasta water as needed.

Divide the pasta among warm bowls. Top each portion with some of the Garlic Chile Oil. Serve immediately.

Maccu

SICILIAN FAVA BEAN STEW WITH FUSILLI

. . . .

In the rural Sicilian kitchen of an American expatriate who insisted she wasn't a good cook, my husband and I ate this delicious pasta dish for lunch, followed by a green salad with paper-thin slices of lemon and fennel. *Maccu*, a fava bean puree made with fresh beans in spring and dried beans the rest of the year, is as common on the Sicilian table as mashed potatoes are in America and equally beloved as comfort food. Sicilians would use wild fennel, which I encourage you to substitute if you have access to it. It is more pungent and haunting in flavor than cultivated fennel. Alternatively, purchase bulb fennel with the feathery leaves attached; use the leaves in this recipe and save the bulb for a salad.

Because fava beans are starchy, the sauce will thicken a lot as it cools. Be sure to leave the sauce on the brothy side so the finished dish isn't too stiff. **Serves 4 to 6**

. . . .

4 pounds fresh fava beans

⅓ cup extra-virgin olive oil, plus more for drizzling

3 large cloves garlic, minced

Pinch of hot pepper flakes

6 green onions, sliced

⅓ cup chopped fresh fennel leaves

Salt and freshly ground black pepper

1 pound fusilli

Freshly grated aged pecorino cheese

Have ready a bowl of ice water. Shell the fava beans. Bring a large pot of water to a boil over high heat. Add the shelled beans and blanch for 30 seconds to 1 minute, depending on their size, then drain and transfer them to the ice water. When cool, drain again. Peel the beans; the skin should slip off easily. You should have 1½ to 2 cups.

Combine the olive oil, garlic, and hot pepper flakes in a skillet and cook over moderate heat until the garlic is fragrant. Add the fava beans, the green onions, and the fennel leaves. Stir well, then add enough water to cover the beans (1½ to 2 cups) and a generous pinch of salt. Bring to a simmer, adjust the heat to maintain a steady simmer, and cook the beans uncovered, stirring often. Add more water as needed to keep the beans covered. In about 1 hour, the beans should be completely tender and mostly whole, although some will have collapsed and thickened the broth. The beans should be on the brothy side. Season with salt and pepper to taste.

Bring a large pot of salted water to a boil over high heat. Add the pasta and cook until al dente. Set aside 1 cup of the pasta water, then drain the pasta and return it to the warm pot over low heat. Add the fava bean sauce and stir well, moistening with some of the reserved pasta water as needed. Try to keep the sauce loose at this point because it thickens as it cools. Divide the pasta among warm bowls and top each portion with a drizzle of olive oil and some of the cheese.

BUTTERFLY PASTA WITH PEAS, TOMATOES, SAUSAGE, AND CREAM

This is a luscious and simple sauce, definitely one of my everyday favorites. The cream softens the edges of the tomato sauce without making it overly rich. Of course, my preference is to use just-picked fresh peas, but they are a fleeting pleasure. Using frozen petite peas will allow you to enjoy this sauce more than just a few weeks a year. **Serves 4 to 6**

¼ cup extra-virgin olive oil

1 yellow onion, minced

4 to 6 ounces hot Italian sausage, preferably with fennel seed

1 pound ripe plum tomatoes, grated (page 25)

¼ cup heavy cream

Salt and freshly ground black pepper

2 pounds English peas, shelled (about 2 cups)

1 pound farfalle, gemelli, or fusilli

¼ cup freshly grated Parmesan cheese

Bring a large pot of salted water to a boil over high heat.

Heat the olive oil in a skillet over moderately low heat. Add the onion and cook until soft, about 10 minutes. Remove the sausage from its casing if necessary and add it to the skillet, breaking it up with a fork. Cook just until it loses most of its pinkness, then add the tomatoes and simmer gently until the tomatoes are softened and no longer raw-tasting, about 5 minutes. Stir in the cream and remove from the heat. Season with salt and pepper to taste.

Put the peas in a sieve that fits inside the pot of water, resting on the edges of the pot, and cook them in the boiling water until tender, about 5 minutes. Lift them out and add them to the skillet. Keep the cooking water at a boil.

Add the pasta to the boiling water and cook until 1 minute shy of al dente. Set aside 1 cup of the pasta water, then drain the pasta and return it to the warm pot over moderately low heat. Add the sauce and cook for about 1 minute to allow the pasta to absorb some of the flavor of the sauce. Moisten with some of the reserved pasta water as needed. Stir in the cheese, then divide among warm bowls and serve immediately.

Spaghetti Spezzati con Piselli

"BROKEN-UP" SPAGHETTI WITH PEAS

At Il Majore, a restaurant that specializes in pork in the Sicilian hill town of Chiaramonte Gulfi, I watched a lone, well-dressed man at the neighboring table savor a lunch of brothy pasta with peas. I decided he was a local businessman who ate there often, and on that day his jaded palate wanted something utterly basic and comforting. Although the dish wasn't on the recited menu—probably because it was seen as too humble to offer visitors—I asked to have it, too.

Cooking the pasta with the peas produces a much more savory dish than if they were cooked separately. The peas, onions, and herbs impart flavor to the cooking water, which the pasta soaks up and gently thickens.

Don't serve the dish immediately. It benefits greatly from standing, allowing the flavors to equalize and the pasta to absorb any remaining liquid. It will stay hot. **Serves 4 to 6**

8 tablespoons extra-virgin olive oil	Heat 6 tablespoons of the olive oil in a large pot over moderately low heat. Add the onion and hot pepper flakes and sauté until the onion is soft, about 10 minutes. Add the peas, spaghetti, basil, and 6 cups water. Season with salt to taste. Bring to a simmer, cover partially, and adjust the heat to maintain a gentle simmer.
1 small yellow onion, minced	
Generous pinch of hot pepper flakes	
4 pounds English peas, shelled (about 4 cups)	Cook, stirring occasionally, until the pasta and peas are tender, about 15 minutes. The pasta should absorb almost all of the liquid, but the dish should not be dry.
1 pound spaghetti, broken in fourths	
2 or 3 fresh basil sprigs	Cover completely, remove from the heat, and let stand for 15 to 20 minutes. Stir in the remaining 2 tablespoons olive oil and taste for salt. You don't need to remove the basil sprigs, as they will be quite soft. Serve the pasta in warm bowls.
Salt	

For the pasta lover, summer brings the return of tomato sauces made with ripe, field-grown tomatoes and basil. These worthy tomatoes inspire sauces of infinite variety: seasoned with fennel sausage, dolloped with ricotta, or heightened with anchovy and capers.

Nature in its wisdom saw to it that almost every summer vegetable likes a tomato sauce. Early in the season, I'll braise zucchini in tomato sauce with anchovies and capers to toss with spaghetti, or soften green beans in a tomato sauce for bucatini. Later, eggplant beckons to be simmered in a tomato sauce with oregano and anchovies. When sweet bell peppers arrive at the end of the season, I pair them with tomatoes, too. One of my favorite sauces, encountered in Italy, is a creamy and richly colored puree of yellow bell peppers and tomato.

Among the few summer sauces I make that don't rely on tomatoes are two delightful ones: a sauce of slow-cooked onions, oregano, and pecorino; and a juicy stew of braised red bell peppers and prosciutto that I particularly like with mafaldine, the wide dried pasta ribbons with a rippled edge (see page 60).

Before summer ends, I spend a few weekends canning or freezing tomato puree (page 25) from homegrown plum tomatoes or those from the farmers' market. Thus provisioned, like the ant in the fable, I feel ready for winter.

summer recipes

PASTA WITH EGGPLANT, TOMATOES, AND RED BELL PEPPERS

Siracusa is one of Sicily's most delightful towns, with a charming old quarter, busy outdoor cafés, a seaside promenade, and a splendid main piazza that's a backdrop for concerts and the nightly *passeggiata* (stroll). Another adaptation from *La Pasta Siciliana* (page 40), this recipe incorporates many of the ingredients that turn up repeatedly in Siracusan cooking: eggplant, anchovies, capers, olives. The fried eggplant all but dissolves in the sauce, but that's just fine. **Serves 4 to 6**

½ pound eggplant (see Note)

Salt

⅓ cup extra-virgin olive oil

2 or 3 large cloves garlic, minced

Pinch of hot pepper flakes

1¼ pounds ripe plum tomatoes, grated (page 25)

24 fresh basil leaves, torn into small pieces

1 large red bell pepper, roasted (page 63), peeled, and seeded, in ¼-inch dice

3 tablespoons pitted and coarsely chopped black olives

1 tablespoon salt-packed capers, well rinsed and coarsely chopped

1 tablespoon very finely minced anchovies

1 pound fusilli, gemelli, penne rigate, or other short dried pasta

⅓ cup freshly grated aged pecorino cheese, plus more for passing at the table

Cut the unpeeled eggplant into 3/4-inch dice. Put it in a sieve set over the sink and sprinkle with 1½ teaspoons salt. Toss well with your hands, then let stand for 1 hour, tossing once or twice more. Pat dry on paper towels (do not rinse first).

Heat the olive oil in a large skillet over moderately high heat. When the oil is almost smoking, add the eggplant. Cook, stirring often, until the eggplant is nicely browned on all sides, about 5 minutes, adjusting the heat if needed to keep it from burning. Reduce the heat to moderate, add the garlic and hot pepper flakes, and cook briefly to release the garlic fragrance; do not let the garlic burn. Add the tomatoes and basil and bring to a simmer. Cook briskly, stirring often and adding water if the mixture threatens to cook dry, until the tomatoes have reduced to a saucelike consistency, about 5 minutes. Stir in the bell pepper and cook for another minute or two to blend the flavors. Stir in the olives, capers, and anchovies. Thin the sauce with water as needed. Taste and adjust the seasoning. Keep warm over low heat.

Bring a large pot of salted water to a boil over high heat. Add the pasta and cook until al dente. Set aside 1 cup of the pasta water, then drain the pasta and return it to the warm pot over low heat. Add the sauce and toss well, moistening with some of the reserved pasta water as needed. Add the cheese and toss again. Divide among warm bowls and serve immediately. Pass the additional cheese at the table.

NOTE: If possible, choose slender, elongated eggplants—often referred to as Asian or Italian eggplant—over the large globe types. Globe eggplants tend to be seedier and spongier, with tougher skin.

CORKSCREW PASTA WITH EGGPLANT, TOMATOES, AND ANCHOVIES

A spoonful of minced anchovies can deepen the flavor of a tomato sauce without making it taste strong or fishy. Perhaps that's because anchovies are high in *umami*, the purported "fifth taste" (along with sweet, sour, salty, and bitter), which some describe as "savoriness." They certainly add a savory background note here; I can't keep my tasting spoon out of the pan. **Serves 4 to 6**

1 pound eggplant (see Note, page 53)

Salt

½ cup extra-virgin olive oil

4 cloves garlic, minced

Pinch of hot pepper flakes

1½ pounds ripe plum tomatoes, grated (page 25)

1½ teaspoons dried oregano

6 to 8 anchovy fillets, minced to a paste

1 pound cavatappi, fusilli, or penne rigate

Cut the unpeeled eggplant into 3/4-inch dice. Put it in a sieve set over the sink and sprinkle with 1 tablespoon salt. Toss well with your hands, then let stand for 1 hour, tossing once or twice more. Pat dry on paper towels (do not rinse first).

Heat the olive oil in a large skillet over moderately high heat. When the oil is almost smoking, add the eggplant. (If necessary, fry the eggplant in batches to avoid overcrowding the skillet.) Cook, stirring often, until the eggplant is nicely browned on all sides, about 5 minutes. Transfer with a slotted spoon to paper towels to drain.

Add the garlic and hot pepper flakes to the skillet and let sizzle until the garlic starts to color. Add the tomatoes and the oregano, crushing the herb between your fingers to release its fragrance. Bring to a simmer, adjust the heat to maintain a gentle simmer, and cook until the sauce is thick, smooth, and flavorful, 15 to 20 minutes. Add 1 or 2 tablespoons of water occasionally to loosen the sauce and help soften the tomatoes. Remove from the heat and stir in the anchovies and the eggplant. Taste and adjust the seasoning.

Bring a large pot of salted water to a boil over high heat. Add the pasta and cook until al dente. Set aside 1 cup of the pasta water, then drain the pasta and return it to the warm pot over low heat. Add the sauce and toss gently so as not to break up the eggplant, moistening with some of the reserved pasta water as needed. Serve immediately in warm bowls.

FRESH RIBBON PASTA WITH GREEN BEANS AND PESTO

Because chopped basil oxidizes so quickly, pesto is best when freshly made. Yes, you can freeze it, but freezing compromises the taste. If you make the pesto and use it immediately, you will notice the difference.

This dish is not about al dente green beans. Cook them until they are soft enough to twirl with the pasta. **Serves 4 to 6**

For the Pesto:

1½ cups firmly packed fresh basil leaves

¼ cup pine nuts, lightly toasted (page 24)

2 cloves garlic, thinly sliced

½ cup extra-virgin olive oil

3 tablespoons freshly grated Parmesan cheese

3 tablespoons freshly grated aged pecorino cheese

Salt

¾ pound haricots verts (slender French green beans), ends trimmed

1 pound Fresh Egg Pasta (page 14), cut as trenette (page 18)

To make the pesto, in a food processor, combine the basil, pine nuts, and garlic and pulse until well chopped. With the machine running, add the olive oil gradually, stopping to scrape down the sides of the bowl once or twice. Puree until almost smooth; the pesto should have a little texture to it. Transfer the mixture to a bowl and stir in the cheeses. Season generously with salt.

Bring a large pot of salted water to a boil over high heat. Add the beans and cook until almost tender, 8 to 10 minutes, depending on their size. Add the pasta and cook until it is al dente.

Just before the pasta is ready, whisk a few tablespoons of hot pasta water into the pesto to thin it. Set aside 1 cup of the pasta water, then drain the pasta and beans and return them to the warm pot. Add the pesto and toss well, moistening with some of the reserved pasta water as needed. Divide among warm bowls and serve immediately.

LONG PIERCED PASTA WITH GREEN BEANS, TOMATOES, AND RICOTTA SALATA

At the restaurant Al Fornello da Ricci, in the town of Ceglie Messapico in Puglia, I had an unusual pasta dish sauced with green beans. Chef Dora Ricci braised the beans in tomato sauce, but what most astonished me was that the beans resembled Chinese long beans. What were they doing in southern Italy?

In fact, Italian seed catalogs, I've since discovered, offer *fagioli rampicanti*, identical to Chinese long beans, also known as "yard-long beans." I have braised them in tomato sauce and tossed them with pasta, as Signora Ricci did, and they are delicious, but I like this version with haricots verts even better. Being tender, the beans cook more quickly and have a fresher taste. **Serves 4 to 6**

6 tablespoons extra-virgin olive oil

4 cloves garlic, minced

Pinch of hot pepper flakes

1¾ pounds ripe plum tomatoes, grated (page 25)

2 to 3 teaspoons dried oregano

Salt

¾ pound haricots verts (slender French green beans), ends trimmed

1 pound bucatini (perciatelli) or spaghetti

¼ pound ricotta salata cheese, coarsely grated

Heat the olive oil in a large skillet over moderate heat. Add the garlic and hot pepper flakes and cook for about 1 minute to release the garlic fragrance. Add the tomatoes and 2 teaspoons of the oregano, crushing the herb between your fingers. Season with salt to taste. Bring to a simmer and adjust the heat to maintain a gentle simmer. Cook, stirring often, until the sauce is thick, smooth, and flavorful, about 15 minutes. Taste halfway through and add the additional oregano, if desired. Add water if the sauce threatens to cook dry before it has the flavor and texture you want.

Bring a large pot of salted water to a boil over high heat. Add the beans and cook until tender, 8 to 10 minutes, depending on their size. Lift them out of the boiling water with a sieve or skimmer and transfer to the sauce. Keep the cooking water at a boil. Cook the beans gently in the sauce for about 5 minutes, adding a little water as needed. Taste and adjust the seasoning.

Add the pasta to the boiling water and cook until about 1 minute shy of al dente. Set aside 1 cup of the pasta water, then drain the pasta and return it to the warm pot over moderately low heat. Add the sauce and cook for about 1 minute to allow the pasta to absorb some of the flavor of the sauce. Moisten with some of the reserved pasta water as needed. Stir in the cheese, then divide among warm bowls and serve immediately.

Maccheroni "Bella Lecce"

PASTA WITH MIXED SUMMER VEGETABLES

Seated in the sterile dining room of the Hotel President in Lecce, a baroque town in Italy's Puglia region, my husband, Doug, and I weren't expecting much. The drab hotel looked like the kind of place where Rotarians might meet for lunch. But when our meal started with divine little rolls punctuated with dry-cured olives, my hopes rose—and they weren't dashed. This pasta dish featuring finely diced summer vegetables, the invention of chef Geraldo Refolo, is still a delicious memory. **Serves 4 to 6**

⅓ cup extra-virgin olive oil

2 ounces pancetta, minced

1 small red onion, minced

3 large cloves garlic, minced

Pinch of hot pepper flakes

1 small yellow, orange, or red bell pepper, seeds and ribs removed, in ¼-inch dice

½ pound eggplant, in ¼-inch dice (see Note, page 53)

½ pound zucchini, in ¼-inch dice

Salt

1½ pounds ripe plum tomatoes, grated (page 25)

12 fresh basil leaves, torn into small pieces

1 pound fusilli, gemelli, penne rigate, or other short dried pasta

½ cup freshly grated aged pecorino cheese, plus more for passing at the table

In a large skillet, heat the olive oil and pancetta over moderately low heat until the pancetta softens and begins to sizzle, 2 to 3 minutes. Add the onion, garlic, and hot pepper flakes and cook until the onion is soft, about 10 minutes. Add the bell pepper, eggplant, and zucchini. Season with salt to taste and cook until the vegetables are slightly softened, about 3 minutes. Add the tomatoes and basil and simmer gently until the vegetables are tender and the tomatoes have reduced to a saucelike consistency, about 15 minutes. Taste and adjust the seasoning.

Bring a large pot of salted water to a boil over high heat. Add the pasta and cook until al dente. Set aside 1 cup of the pasta water, then drain the pasta and return it to the warm pot over low heat. Add the sauce and toss well, moistening with some of the reserved pasta water as needed. Add the cheese and toss again. Divide among warm bowls and serve immediately. Pass the additional cheese at the table.

DRIED RIBBON PASTA WITH RED BELL PEPPERS AND PROSCIUTTO

Whenever I shop at a specialty-food store or an Italian deli, I check the shelves for unfamiliar dried pasta shapes. That's how I found mafaldine, which are 1/2-inch-wide ribbons of pasta with ruffled edges. The broader mafalde, which look like lasagne noodles with rippled edges, are perhaps better known, but narrower mafaldine are easier to twirl around softened sweet bell peppers. Delverde, the prominent Italian pasta manufacturer, makes mafaldine. Ask your merchant to order them, or substitute dried linguine.

You'll need at least a 12-inch skillet to handle all these peppers. I don't roast and peel the peppers first because I don't want to lose a drop of their flavorful juices. I don't mind the paper-thin skins, and the juices contribute to a luscious sauce. **Serves 4 to 6**

3 tablespoons extra-virgin olive oil

4 large cloves garlic, minced

5 large red bell peppers, seeds and ribs removed, sliced 1/4 inch wide

1 1/2 teaspoons dried oregano

Salt

3 to 4 ounces prosciutto, minced

1 pound mafaldine, linguine, or spaghetti

2 tablespoons unsalted butter

2 tablespoons chopped fresh Italian (flat-leaf) parsley

In a large skillet, heat the olive oil over moderate heat. Add the garlic and cook briefly to release its fragrance. Add the bell peppers and oregano, crushing the herb between your fingers. Season with salt to taste. Cover and reduce the heat to moderately low. Cook gently, stirring occasionally, until the peppers are tender but not mushy, 30 to 40 minutes. Stir in the prosciutto and a few tablespoons of water to loosen the pan juices, then remove from the heat.

Bring a large pot of salted water to a boil over high heat. Add the pasta and cook until al dente. Set aside 1 cup of the pasta water, then drain the pasta and return it to the warm pot over low heat. Add the sauce, butter, and parsley and toss until the butter melts, moistening with some of the reserved pasta water as needed. Serve immediately in warm bowls.

PASTA WITH A CREAMY YELLOW BELL PEPPER AND TOMATO SAUCE

Traveling in the off-season in Puglia, one of Italy's least-visited regions, I figured that my husband and I could be somewhat spontaneous about where we stayed. But when I called the Masseria Il Frantoio near Ostuni a couple of days before we planned to arrive, I learned that the tiny rural inn would have no room for us. My disappointment must have been audible, because owner Armando Balestrazzi invited us to come for dinner at least. His wife Rosalba proved to be a fabulous cook, and this pasta dish was on the menu. She called it *penne saporite* ("flavorful penne"), definitely an understatement. **Serves 4 to 6**

1/3 cup extra-virgin olive oil

1 small red onion, minced

2 large cloves garlic, minced

Pinch of hot pepper flakes

1 small yellow or orange bell pepper, seeds and ribs removed, in 1/4-inch dice

1 pound ripe plum tomatoes, grated (page 25)

Salt

12 fresh basil leaves, torn into small pieces

1 pound penne rigate or fusilli

1/3 cup freshly grated aged pecorino cheese, plus more for passing at the table

Heat the olive oil in a large skillet over moderately low heat. Add the onion and sauté until soft, about 10 minutes. Add the garlic and hot pepper flakes and sauté briefly to release the garlic fragrance. Add the bell pepper, tomatoes, and salt to taste. Cover and simmer gently until the pepper is tender, about 15 minutes.

Puree the sauce until smooth in a food processor or blender, then return it to the skillet. Add the basil, then reheat the sauce over low heat. You will probably need to add 1/2 cup or more of water to thin the sauce to a desirable consistency. Taste and adjust the seasoning. Keep warm.

Bring a large pot of salted water to a boil over high heat. Add the pasta and cook until al dente. Set aside 1 cup of the pasta water, then drain the pasta and return it to the warm pot over low heat. Add the sauce and cheese and toss, moistening with some of the reserved pasta water as needed. Divide among warm bowls and serve immediately. Pass the additional cheese at the table.

"TWINS" PASTA WITH GREEN BELL PEPPERS, SAUSAGE, AND TOMATOES

Although green bell peppers have fallen out of favor—overshadowed by their sweeter, riper, red and orange counterparts—I'm still a fan. I like that pronounced grassy, green-bean character that dominates before the sugar develops. Roast and peel them, then braise them briefly in tomato sauce with crumbled sausage for a rustic dinner. **Serves 4 to 6**

2 green bell peppers

¼ cup extra-virgin olive oil

2 large cloves garlic, minced

Approximately 6 ounces hot Italian sausage, preferably with fennel seed

¾ pound ripe plum tomatoes, peeled, seeded, and diced

Hot pepper flakes (optional)

Salt

1 pound gemelli, cavatappi, or fusilli

¼ pound ricotta salata cheese

Roast the bell peppers over a gas flame or under a broiler until the skin is blackened all over. When cool enough to handle, peel the peppers, removing all traces of blackened skin without rinsing them. Halve the peppers and remove the stem, seeds, and ribs. Slice thinly.

Heat the olive oil in a large skillet over moderately low heat. Add the garlic and cook briefly to release its fragrance. Remove the sausage from its casing if necessary and add it to the skillet, breaking it up with a fork. Cook just until it loses most of its pinkness. Add the tomatoes and cook gently until they are slightly softened, about 5 minutes. Taste and add hot pepper flakes to taste, if desired. Stir in the bell peppers and salt to taste. Cook gently for about 5 minutes to blend the flavors.

Bring a large pot of salted water to a boil over high heat. Add the pasta and cook until about 1 minute shy of al dente. Set aside 1 cup of the pasta water, then drain the pasta and return it to the warm pot over moderately low heat. Add the sauce and cook for about 1 minute to allow the pasta to absorb some of the flavor of the sauce. Moisten with some of the reserved pasta water as needed.

Remove from the heat and, using the coarse side of a box grater, grate the cheese directly into the pot. Stir again, then divide among warm bowls and serve immediately.

LONG PIERCED PASTA WITH ONIONS, OREGANO, AND PECORINO

With slow cooking, sliced onions become supersweet and meltingly soft, the foundation of a simple pasta sauce. They need only some sharp pecorino and coarsely ground black pepper to balance their sweetness.

Note the technique used for slicing the onions—lengthwise instead of crosswise. This method produces slices of approximately equal length, whereas slicing the onion halves crosswise—the usual method—yields short and long strands. **Serves 4 to 6**

2 pounds yellow onions

6 tablespoons extra-virgin olive oil

1 tablespoon dried oregano

Salt and coarsely ground black pepper (see Note)

1 pound bucatini (perciatelli) or spaghetti

1 cup freshly grated aged pecorino cheese

Cut the ends off the onions, halve the onions lengthwise (through the ends), and peel. Slice thinly from tip end to root end. Heat the olive oil in a large skillet over moderate heat. Add the onions and oregano, crushing the herb between your fingers to release its fragrance. Season with salt to taste. Cook, tossing to coat the onions with the oil, until they wilt slightly, about 5 minutes. Then cover, reduce heat to low, and cook, stirring occasionally until the onions are very soft and sweet, about 1 hour.

Bring a large pot of salted water to a boil over high heat. Add the pasta and cook until about 1 minute shy of al dente. Set aside 1 cup of the pasta water, then drain the pasta and return it to the warm pot over low heat. Add the onion sauce, the cheese, and a generous amount of pepper. Toss well, moistening with some of the reserved pasta water as needed. Divide among warm bowls and serve immediately.

NOTE: To make coarsely ground pepper, pound whole peppercorns in a mortar with a pestle, or adjust your pepper mill to produce a coarse grind.

Orecchiette alla Foggiana

EAR-SHAPED PASTA WITH POTATOES AND ARUGULA

At a fish restaurant near Termoli in Italy's Molise region, my husband, Doug, and I ate a parade of impeccable seafood antipasti followed by this pasta dish. Having just spent three weeks in Puglia, we thought we had eaten orecchiette every possible way, but this sauce was new to us and delicious. The restaurant's Pugliese owner said that the preparation is traditional in her hometown of Foggia.

Serves 4 to 6

⅓ cup extra-virgin olive oil

2 large cloves garlic, minced

Pinch of hot pepper flakes

1¼ pounds ripe plum tomatoes, grated (page 25)

Salt

6 ounces baby arugula, left whole, or larger arugula, stems removed and leaves coarsely chopped

1 pound russet (baking) potatoes, peeled, in ½-inch dice

1 pound orecchiette

Heat the olive oil in a large skillet over moderate heat. Add the garlic and hot pepper flakes and cook for about 1 minute to release the garlic fragrance. Add the tomatoes and salt to taste. Cook, stirring often, until the tomatoes soften and become sauce-like, 15 to 20 minutes, adding water when the tomatoes threaten to cook dry. Stir in the arugula and cook just until it wilts, about 1 minute.

Bring a large pot of salted water to a boil over high heat. Add the potatoes and pasta and cook until the pasta is al dente. Set aside 1 cup of the pasta water, then drain the pasta and potatoes and return them to the warm pot over low heat. Add the sauce and stir gently to avoid breaking up the potatoes. Moisten with some of the reserved pasta water as needed. Divide among warm bowls and serve immediately.

PASTA WITH A PESTO OF ALMONDS, TOMATOES, CAPERS, ANCHOVIES, GARLIC, AND BASIL

Visiting Lipari, the Aeolian island off the coast of Sicily, my husband, Doug, and I tried the strategy of seeking out the busiest restaurant for our lunch. To our surprise, all the simple trattorias in the heart of Lipari town were virtually empty. Where was everybody?

We finally found a bustling dining room at Filippino, a nearly century-old hilltop restaurant that I had mistakenly thought was a tourist trap. The pleasant setting does indeed draw tourists, but the cooking is excellent.

Chef Lucio Bernardi gave me the recipe for the dish I ordered, which was named for one of its chief ingredients: capers, the "orchids" of the Aeolian islands. A blend of uncooked tomatoes, almonds, anchovies, capers, and herbs, it closely resembles the famous pesto of Trapani, another Sicilian waterfront town. **Serves 4 to 6**

3 tablespoons blanched (skinless) almonds

1 pound tomatoes, halved and seeded (no need to peel)

¼ cup salt-packed capers, well rinsed

4 anchovy fillets

2 cloves garlic

20 fresh basil leaves

5 fresh mint leaves

1 Calabrian chile (page 23) or a pinch of hot pepper flakes

⅓ cup extra-virgin olive oil

¼ cup freshly grated aged pecorino cheese

Salt

1 pound penne rigate, gemelli, or fusilli

Place the almonds in a food processor and pulse until finely chopped. Add the tomatoes, capers, anchovies, garlic, basil, mint, and chile and puree until smooth. With the machine running, add the olive oil gradually.

Transfer the sauce to a bowl and stir in the cheese. Season with salt to taste.

Bring a large pot of salted water to a boil over high heat. Add the pasta and cook until al dente. Set aside 1 cup of the pasta water, then drain. Put the pasta in a serving bowl and add as much of the sauce as you like—you may not need it all. Toss well, moistening with some of the reserved pasta water as needed. Serve immediately.

SPAGHETTI WITH CAPERS, TOMATOES, AND ALMONDS

The picturesque Aeolian island of Salina, off the northeast coast of Sicily, produces superb capers that rival the better-known product of Pantelleria. My husband, Doug, and I visited Salina in mid-May, when the caper harvest was just beginning, and we spotted a few locals making the first pass through their caper bushes. The harvest lasts until September, and workers must go through the bushes every few days to pick the capers, which are flower buds, at just the right size.

Not surprisingly, capers are lavishly used in the local cooking, as in this re-creation of a dish I enjoyed at the charming Hotel Signum, where we stayed. Salt-packed, not brine-packed, capers are a must. **Serves 4 to 6**

⅓ cup extra-virgin olive oil

3 large cloves garlic, finely minced

Pinch of hot pepper flakes

¾ pound ripe plum tomatoes, grated (page 25)

3 tablespoons salt-packed capers, well rinsed and very finely minced

¼ cup finely ground toasted almonds (page 24)

Salt

1 pound spaghetti

Bring a large pot of salted water to a boil over high heat.

Heat the olive oil in a skillet over moderately low heat. Add the garlic and hot pepper flakes and cook until the garlic just begins to color. Add the tomatoes and simmer until soft, about 10 minutes, adding a few tablespoons of hot water from the pasta pot to make the mixture more saucelike as needed. Don't worry if the tomato and oil look separated at this point; the almonds will bring the sauce together.

Stir the capers and almonds into the sauce and season with salt to taste. Stir in a few more tablespoons hot pasta water as needed to make a smooth and creamy sauce.

Add the pasta to the boiling water and cook until al dente. Set aside 1 cup of the pasta water, then drain the pasta and return it to the warm pot over low heat. Add the sauce to the pasta and toss well, moistening with some of the reserved pasta water as needed. Divide among warm bowls and serve immediately.

LONG PIERCED PASTA WITH SLOW-ROASTED TOMATOES

Roasting tomatoes slowly in a low oven produces a deep, intense, almost caramelized flavor that's completely unlike the taste of tomatoes simmered briskly on the stove. Although slow roasting takes a while, it is unattended cooking. At mealtime, all you have to do is chop and season these concentrated tomatoes, and you have a memorable sauce. **Serves 4 to 6**

1¾ to 2 pounds ripe plum tomatoes that feel heavy for their size

⅓ cup extra-virgin olive oil

3 cloves garlic, minced

Salt

1 or 2 Calabrian chiles, finely minced (page 23)

24 fresh basil leaves, torn into small pieces

1 pound bucatini (perciatelli) or spaghetti

⅓ cup freshly grated aged pecorino cheese, plus more for passing at the table

Preheat the oven to 300°F. Cut the tomatoes in half lengthwise and arrange them, cut side up, in a baking dish just large enough to hold them in one layer. Spoon the olive oil over and dot the surface of the tomatoes with the garlic, dividing it evenly. Season well with salt.

Bake the tomatoes, basting occasionally with the oil in the baking dish, until they are very soft and somewhat shriveled, about 3 hours. Transfer the tomatoes to a cutting board and chop well, then put the tomatoes and any oil from the baking dish into a serving bowl. Stir in the chiles and basil. Taste and add more salt if needed.

Bring a large pot of salted water to a boil over high heat. Add the pasta and cook until al dente, then drain the pasta and add it to the serving bowl. Add the cheese and toss well. Divide among warm bowls and serve immediately, passing the additional cheese at the table.

SPAGHETTI WITH MARINATED TOMATOES, ARUGULA, AND RICOTTA SALATA

A salad of marinated tomatoes and arugula makes a fast pasta sauce that appeals to appetites diminished by heat. I don't even warm the pasta bowls. **Serves 4 to 6**

1½ pounds ripe slicing tomatoes, peeled and seeded (page 26), then thinly sliced

⅓ cup extra-virgin olive oil

2 cloves garlic, minced

2 Calabrian chiles (page 23), minced, or a pinch of hot pepper flakes

Salt

1 pound spaghetti

⅓ pound baby arugula

¼ pound ricotta salata cheese, coarsely grated

In a large serving bowl, combine the tomatoes, olive oil, garlic, chiles, and salt to taste. You can do this step a couple of hours ahead; keep at room temperature.

Bring a large pot of salted water to a boil over high heat. Add the pasta and cook until al dente.

Just before the pasta is done, put the arugula in the serving bowl. Drain the pasta and add it to the bowl along with the cheese. Toss until the arugula wilts slightly, then serve immediately.

RIGATONI WITH SPICY TOMATO SAUCE AND FRESH RICOTTA

Opting to follow the crowds instead of the guidebooks, my husband, Doug, and I ended up in a packed working-class lunch spot in Naples one day. After a glance around, we decided to have what everyone else was having: rigatoni in tomato sauce topped with a dollop of snow-white ricotta, followed by sautéed *friarielle*, a dialect name for broccoli rabe, and cool, crisp grapes for dessert. **Serves 4 to 6**

⅓ cup extra-virgin olive oil

4 cloves garlic, minced

4 tablespoons minced fresh Italian (flat-leaf) parsley

Pinch of hot pepper flakes

2 pounds ripe plum tomatoes, grated (see page 25)

Salt and freshly ground black pepper

½ cup whole-milk ricotta, at room temperature

1 pound rigatoni or penne rigate

Heat the olive oil in a large skillet over moderate heat. Add the garlic, 3 tablespoons of the parsley, and the hot pepper flakes and cook briefly to release the fragrance of the seasonings. Add the tomatoes, season with salt to taste, and bring to a simmer. Adjust the heat to maintain a gentle simmer and cook until the sauce is thick and flavorful, about 20 minutes. If it threatens to cook dry before the flavors have melded, add a little water and continue simmering.

In a bowl, whisk the ricotta until smooth. Season with salt and black pepper to taste.

Bring a large pot of salted water to a boil over high heat. Add the pasta and cook until about 1 minute shy of al dente. Remove 1 cup of pasta water, then drain the pasta and return it to the warm pot over moderately low heat. Add the tomato sauce and cook for about 1 minute to allow the pasta to absorb some of the flavor of the sauce. Moisten with a little of the reserved pasta water as needed.

Divide the pasta among warm bowls. Top each portion with a dollop of ricotta and a sprinkle of the remaining 1 tablespoon parsley. Serve immediately.

SPIRAL PASTA WITH TOMATOES AND MOZZARELLA

The molten mozzarella makes this dish hard to eat gracefully, so save it for close friends and casual evenings. Serve and eat it quickly, before the nuggets of mozzarella cool and lose their charm. **Serves 4 to 6**

⅓ cup extra-virgin olive oil

4 cloves garlic, minced

Pinch of hot pepper flakes

1¾ pounds ripe plum tomatoes, grated (page 25)

Salt

1 tablespoon dried oregano

1 pound fusilli or penne rigate

½ pound whole-milk mozzarella, in ½-inch cubes

Freshly grated aged pecorino cheese (optional)

Heat the olive oil in a large skillet over moderately low heat. Add the garlic and hot pepper flakes and cook until the garlic begins to color. Add the tomatoes and a generous pinch of salt. Add the oregano, crushing it between your fingers to release its fragrance. Bring to a simmer, adjust the heat to maintain a gentle simmer, and cook until the sauce is thick, smooth, and flavorful, 15 to 20 minutes. Add 1 or 2 tablespoons of water occasionally to loosen the sauce and help soften the tomatoes.

Bring a large pot of salted water to a boil over high heat. Add the pasta and cook until about 1 minute shy of al dente. Set aside 1 cup of the pasta water, then drain the pasta and return it to the warm pot over moderately low heat. Add the sauce and cook for about 1 minute to allow the pasta to absorb some of the flavor of the sauce. Moisten with some of the reserved pasta water as needed.

Remove the pot from the heat, add the mozzarella without stirring, and cover the pot. Let stand for 1 minute, then divide the pasta among warm bowls and serve immediately. Pass pecorino at the table for those who want it.

SPAGHETTI WITH ZUCCHINI, TOMATOES, ANCHOVIES, AND CAPERS

Another gem of a recipe adapted from *La Pasta Siciliana* (page 40). **Serves 4 to 6**

⅓ cup extra-virgin olive oil

1 pound small zucchini, in ¼-inch dice

Salt

2 large cloves garlic, minced

1½ pounds ripe plum tomatoes, halved, seeded, and chopped

Pinch of hot pepper flakes

4 anchovy fillets, minced to a paste

2 tablespoons salt-packed capers, well rinsed and chopped

16 black olives, pitted, each cut into 4 to 6 pieces

16 fresh basil leaves, torn into small pieces

1 pound spaghetti

Heat the olive oil in a large skillet over moderate heat. Add the zucchini, season with salt to taste, and cook, stirring often, until the zucchini soften and begin to color, about 5 minutes.

Add the garlic and cook for about 1 minute to release its fragrance. Add the tomatoes and hot pepper flakes. Adjust the heat to maintain a gentle simmer and cook, stirring often, until the tomatoes collapse and form a thick sauce, 10 to 15 minutes. Add 1 or 2 tablespoons of water occasionally if the mixture threatens to cook dry. Stir in the anchovies, capers, olives, and basil.

Bring a large pot of salted water to a boil over high heat. Add the pasta and cook until about 1 minute shy of al dente. Set aside 1 cup of the pasta water, then drain the pasta and return it to the warm pot over moderately low heat. Add the sauce and cook for about 1 minute to allow the pasta to absorb some of the flavor of the sauce. Moisten with some of the reserved pasta water as needed. Divide among warm bowls and serve immediately.

TONY TERLATO'S ZUCCHINI LINGUINE

Tony Terlato is my husband's boss and an enthusiastic pasta cook of Sicilian heritage. He often makes this dish with overgrown zucchini, which he cuts in half lengthwise and slices into half moons after scooping out the seeds. My feeling is that any dish that's good with gonzo zucchini will be even better with young, tender squash.

Being in the wine business, Tony naturally has a wine recommendation for his dish: Fiano di Avellino, a fragrant white wine from Campania, and preferably the brand he sells. **Serves 4 to 6**

¾ cup extra-virgin olive oil

1½ pounds small zucchini, ends trimmed, sliced into ¼-inch-thick rounds

Salt

1 pound linguine

2 tablespoons unsalted butter

24 fresh basil leaves, torn into small pieces

Pinch of hot pepper flakes

⅔ cup freshly grated Parmesan or aged pecorino cheese

Bring a large pot of salted water to a boil over high heat.

Heat the olive oil in a large skillet over moderately high heat. Add the zucchini in batches; do not crowd the pan. Fry until the zucchini rounds are golden on the bottom, about 5 minutes, then turn with 2 forks and fry until the second side is golden, 3 to 4 minutes longer. Transfer to paper towels to drain. Sprinkle with salt to taste while hot. Reserve the frying oil.

Add the pasta to the boiling water and cook until al dente. Set aside 1 cup of the pasta water, then drain the pasta and return it to the warm pot over low heat. Add the butter, basil, hot pepper flakes, and 3 tablespoons of the frying oil. Toss well, then add the zucchini and cheese and toss again gently, moistening with some of the reserved pasta water as needed. Serve immediately in warm bowls.

Compared to summer's *abbondanza,* autumn is quieter in the pasta kitchen. The harvest slows, a welcome breather after August and September when gardens and markets are so profuse that a cook can almost hyperventilate. It's a relief not to face mountains of perishable produce that has to be used *right now.*

For me, the peak autumn experience is cooking with fresh shell beans such as cranberry and lima beans. Of all the autumn vegetables, these are the most fleeting. When they're gone, they're gone for a year. I make brothy sauces with them for cavatelli and orecchiette, two southern Italian pasta shapes popular with beans.

Other cool-weather crops that dominate the autumn market include hard-shelled squashes, Brussels sprouts, leeks, spinach, and, as winter nears, radicchio. The dense-fleshed autumn squashes, especially kabocha and butternut, make a savory ravioli filling, complemented by melted butter and crisp leaves of fried sage. Full-flavored, large-leaved spinach produces beautiful green fettuccine too lovely to sauce with anything heavier than more spinach, butter, and Parmesan.

Pasta lovers can only rejoice at how rapidly radicchio has been embraced by Americans. Once virtually unknown here, then a rarity, it has now become a staple in many urban supermarkets. Shredded and braised with pancetta until it all but melts, it makes a captivating pasta sauce.

autumn recipes

Cavatappi con Cavoli di Bruxelles

CORKSCREW PASTA WITH BRUSSELS SPROUTS, SAUSAGE, TOMATOES, AND CREAM

You will look long and hard to find an Italian pasta sauce with Brussels sprouts—I'm still looking—but that doesn't disqualify them from the pasta realm in my estimation. They are really just little cabbages, so I treat them much as I would cabbage for a pasta sauce, slicing and braising them until tender with a little sausage, tomato, and cream. If you can't find sausage with fennel, add some lightly crushed fennel seed to taste. **Serves 4 to 6**

1 pound Brussels sprouts, ends trimmed

¼ cup extra-virgin olive oil

½ pound hot Italian sausage, preferably with fennel seed

4 large cloves garlic, minced

1 pound ripe plum tomatoes, peeled, seeded, and diced

Salt

¼ cup heavy cream

1 pound cavatappi, fusilli, or farfalle

Bring a large pot of salted water to a boil over high heat. Add the Brussels sprouts (I put them in a sieve that fits inside the pot, resting on the edges, so I can lift them out easily) and cook until they are tender when pierced, about 12 minutes. Lift them out of the boiling water with the sieve or a skimmer and cool under cold running water. Drain well. Halve them, then slice about ¼-inch thick and set aside. Add a little more water to the pot and return to a boil.

Heat the olive oil in a large skillet over moderately low heat. Remove the sausage from its casing if necessary and add it to the skillet, breaking it up with a fork. Cook just until it loses most of its pinkness. Add the garlic and cook for a minute or two to release its fragrance. Add the tomatoes and cook briefly to soften, but don't let them collapse into a sauce.

Add the Brussels sprouts, season with salt to taste, and stir to blend. Stir in the cream. Reduce the heat to low.

Add the pasta to the boiling water and cook until al dente. Set aside 1 cup of the pasta water, then drain the pasta and return it to the warm pot over low heat. Add the sauce and toss well, moistening with some of the reserved pasta water as needed. Divide among warm bowls and serve immediately.

Tonnarelli con Porri

SQUARE-CUT FRESH "SPAGHETTI" WITH LEEKS, TOASTED WALNUTS, AND CREAM

Small portions of this creamy pasta could precede a roast chicken, grilled veal chops, or other simple meat dish without a sauce. You could also simply follow it with salad and fruit for a lighter meal. It needs no cheese; it is rich enough. **Serves 6**

5 or 6 leeks, white and pale green parts only

4 tablespoons unsalted butter

Salt and coarsely ground black pepper (see Note, page 65)

1 cup heavy cream

¾ cup homemade chicken stock or canned low-sodium broth

2 tablespoons minced fresh Italian (flat-leaf) parsley

1 pound Fresh Egg Pasta (page 14), cut as tonnarelli or fettuccine (page 18)

½ cup walnuts, toasted (page 24) and chopped medium fine

Bring a large pot of salted water to a boil over high heat.

Cut the leeks in half lengthwise, then slice thinly crosswise. Fill a sink with cold water, add the sliced leeks, and swish them around vigorously to dislodge any dirt. Lift them out of the water and into a strainer.

Melt the butter in a large skillet over moderately low heat. Add the leeks and season with salt to taste. Stir to coat with the butter. Cover and cook gently until the leeks are tender, about 20 minutes, reducing the heat if necessary. There should be a few tablespoons of flavorful liquid in the skillet at the end.

Stir in the cream and stock and simmer briefly to reduce slightly. Don't over-reduce, as the pasta will absorb a lot of sauce. Stir in the parsley and pepper to taste. Keep warm.

Add the pasta to the boiling water and cook until just shy of al dente. Set aside 1 cup of the pasta water, then drain the pasta and return it to the warm pot over low heat. Add the sauce and the walnuts and cook briefly, tossing constantly, to allow the pasta to absorb some of the sauce. Moisten with some of the reserved pasta water as needed. Divide the pasta among warm bowls and serve immediately.

Tonnarelli alla Boscaiola

SQUARE-CUT FRESH "SPAGHETTI" WITH A SAVORY MUSHROOM SAUCE

Although cultivated mushrooms are available year-round, pasta with a richly seasoned, tomato-based mushroom sauce strikes me as a cool-weather meal. You can use standard supermarket button mushrooms for this recipe or any wild mushrooms you are lucky enough to get. If you use portobello mushrooms, scrape out the dark gills first.

This sauce is equally good on fresh and dried pasta. Pair it with spaghetti or farfalle when you don't want to make the tonnarelli. **Serves 4 to 6**

½ ounce dried porcini

6 tablespoons extra-virgin olive oil

1½ pounds fresh mushrooms (see recipe introduction), ends trimmed, then halved and thinly sliced

Salt and freshly ground black pepper

2 ounces pancetta, minced

½ large yellow onion, minced

1 celery rib, in small, neat dice

1 carrot, in small, neat dice

2 cloves garlic, minced

2 teaspoons minced fresh sage

1 teaspoon minced fresh rosemary

1 pound ripe plum tomatoes, grated (page 25)

1 pound Fresh Egg Pasta (page 14), cut as tonnarelli (page 18), or dried spaghetti or farfalle

⅔ cup freshly grated Parmesan cheese

Soak the porcini in $1\frac{1}{2}$ cups water for 1 hour. Lift out of the soaking liquid with a slotted spoon, leaving any grit behind. Chop the porcini, then strain the liquid through a sieve lined with a damp paper towel. Set the liquid aside.

Heat a very large skillet over high heat. When hot, add 2 tablespoons of the olive oil. When the oil is almost smoking, add the fresh mushrooms. Let sizzle without stirring for a couple of minutes so the mushrooms brown nicely, then stir and continue cooking, stirring infrequently, until the mushrooms are tender and nicely browned all over, about 5 minutes. Season with salt and pepper to taste and transfer to a plate.

Reduce the heat to moderately low. Return the skillet to the heat and add the remaining 4 tablespoons olive oil and the pancetta. Cook briefly until the pancetta begins to crisp, then add the onion, celery, carrot, garlic, sage, and rosemary. Cook slowly until the vegetables are soft, about 15 minutes. Add the tomatoes and chopped porcini and simmer for about 5 minutes to soften the tomatoes, then return the browned mushrooms to the skillet. Add 1 cup of the strained porcini liquid and season with salt and pepper to taste.

Bring to a simmer, cover, and adjust the heat to maintain a gentle simmer. Cook for 15 minutes to blend the flavors. Thin if necessary with the remaining porcini liquid.

(continued)

SQUARE-CUT FRESH "SPAGHETTI" WITH A SAVORY MUSHROOM SAUCE (CONTINUED)

While the sauce is cooking, bring a large pot of salted water to a boil over high heat. Add the pasta and cook until al dente. Set aside 1 cup of the pasta water, then drain the pasta and return it to the warm pot over low heat. Add the sauce and toss, moistening with some of the reserved pasta water as needed. Add half of the cheese and toss again. Divide among warm bowls, topping each portion with some of the remaining cheese. Serve immediately.

Ravioli di Zucca

PUMPKIN RAVIOLI WITH FRIED SAGE

Ravioli are fun to make at home and less work than lasagne or cannelloni because you don't have to boil the pasta before you fill them. If you are painstaking—rolling the pasta very thin and being precise in your work—you will have beautiful ravioli far more delicate than any you can buy.

It is important to make your pasta sheets as straight-edged as possible or you will have to trim them and throw a lot of dough away. Thinness is also critical because the dough is doubled around the filling.

These ravioli are filled with well-seasoned squash puree and sauced simply with melted butter, a shower of Parmesan, and crisp fried sage leaves. They are too delicate to drain. You will need a wire-mesh skimmer or other strainer to lift them out of the boiling pasta water.

Makes about 60 ravioli; serves 10 as a first course or 6 as a main course

For the filling:

1 small butternut squash
(1 to 1½ pounds)

3 tablespoons freshly grated
Parmesan cheese

3 tablespoons fine bread crumbs
(page 21)

Freshly grated nutmeg

Salt

1 large egg yolk

Fresh Egg Pasta (page 14)
made with 2 extra-large eggs
and approximately 1⅔ cups
unbleached all-purpose flour

Semolina for dusting

(continued)

Preheat the oven to 400°F. To make the filling, cut the squash in half lengthwise and scoop out the strings and seeds. Put the squash halves in a baking dish, cut side up. Cover and bake until tender when pierced, about 1 hour. Cool, then scrape the flesh away from the skins. Puree the flesh in a food processor until smooth.

Measure 1 cup squash puree into a bowl. (Discard any remaining puree or reserve for another use.) Add the cheese, bread crumbs, and nutmeg and salt to taste. Stir in the egg yolk.

Roll the pasta on the pasta machine into sheets as thin as you are comfortable working with. (I roll it to number 7, two steps thinner than I do for fettuccine.) Lay the sheets on clean dish towels as you make them.

Prepare the ravioli while the pasta is still fresh and somewhat moist. On a work surface lightly dusted with semolina, lay 1 sheet flat. Dot the sheet with small mounds of filling in two parallel rows, using a scant 1 teaspoon filling for each mound. The mounds should be about 1 inch apart and the rows about 2 inches apart. Keep the mounds far enough from the edges of the dough to allow room to seal the ravioli. With a pastry brush dipped in cold water, lightly moisten the edges of the pasta dough and moisten a strip between the rows.

(continued)

PUMPKIN RAVIOLI WITH FRIED SAGE (CONTINUED)

8 tablespoons unsalted butter

2 tablespoons extra-virgin olive oil

30 large fresh sage leaves

Salt and freshly ground black pepper

¾ to 1 cup freshly grated
Parmesan cheese

Top with another sheet of pasta dough (four hands are helpful here, but not essential), carefully aligning the edges. Press between the mounds and between the rows to seal the ravioli. Use a fluted pastry wheel to cut between the ravioli. Transfer them to semolina-dusted trays or dish towels to rest while you prepare the sauce. If you are not going to cook the ravioli immediately, you need to turn them every 20 minutes or so to prevent them from sticking to the trays or towels.

Bring two large pots of salted water to a boil over high heat.

Meanwhile, prepare the sage leaves: Melt 2 tablespoons of the butter with the olive oil in a large skillet over moderately low heat. Add the sage leaves and cook slowly, turning them occasionally, until they crisp, 5 to 7 minutes. Transfer them to paper towels to drain and sprinkle with salt.

Pour the fat from the pan into a small cup and let the dark particles settle to the bottom, then pour the clear fat back into the skillet. Add the remaining 6 tablespoons butter and melt over low heat. Season to taste with salt and pepper.

Add the ravioli to the boiling water, dividing them between the two pots. Cook until al dente, 3 to 4 minutes, depending on how dry they are and how thin your pasta is. Stir them often so they don't stick to each other. Check by lifting one out with a strainer and cutting off a bit of the edge to taste. When the ravioli are done, lift them out of the pot a few at a time with a skimmer or strainer, letting excess water drip back into the pot. Divide them among warmed bowls, drizzling each portion with the melted butter and sprinkling with some of the cheese and sage leaves. Serve immediately.

Tagliatelle con Radicchio

FRESH RIBBON PASTA WITH BRAISED RADICCHIO, PANCETTA, AND PARMESAN

This recipe is the result of a fortuitous mistake, when I thought I had turned the heat off under the radicchio but I hadn't. The lengthy cooking all but melted the radicchio, merging it with the onion and pancetta until you couldn't tease the parts apart. A brilliant error on my part, I must say. *Tagliatelle* is the Bolognese word for flat ribbon pasta similar to fettuccine. **Serves 4 to 6**

¼ pound pancetta, minced

3 tablespoons extra-virgin olive oil

1 large yellow onion, minced

1 pound radicchio, quartered, cored, and thinly sliced

½ cup dry white wine

Salt and freshly ground black pepper

1 pound Fresh Egg Pasta (page 14), cut as fettuccine (page 18)

2 tablespoons minced fresh Italian (flat-leaf) parsley

4 tablespoons unsalted butter, in 8 pieces

⅓ cup freshly grated Parmesan cheese

Put the pancetta and olive oil in a large skillet and cook over moderately low heat until the pancetta begins to crisp, about 10 minutes. Add the onion and cook, stirring often, until soft and golden, about 10 minutes. Add the radicchio, wine, and salt and pepper to taste. Raise the heat to moderate, bring to a simmer, and cook, stirring, for about 3 minutes to soften the radicchio and allow the alcohol to evaporate. Cover and adjust the heat so the radicchio cooks gently. Cook, stirring occasionally, until the radicchio is meltingly tender, about 30 minutes.

Bring a large pot of salted water to a boil over high heat. Add the pasta and cook until al dente. While the pasta cooks, stir the parsley into the radicchio and add a few tablespoons of the hot pasta water to loosen the sauce.

Set aside 1 cup of the pasta water, then drain the pasta and return it to the warm pot over low heat. Add the butter and toss well, moistening with a little of the reserved pasta water. Add the sauce and the cheese and toss again, moistening with more pasta water as needed. Serve immediately in warm bowls.

Spaghetti con Radicchio alla Piemontese

SPAGHETTI WITH RADICCHIO, GARLIC, ANCHOVIES, AND BREAD CRUMBS

Of the many vegetables that are wonderful dipped in *bagna cauda*—the Piedmontese "hot bath" of anchovies, garlic, and olive oil—radicchio is among the best. No surprise, then, that the same ingredients work as a pasta sauce. To duplicate the mellow flavor of *bagna cauda*, it's important to cook the garlic slowly and to use the best anchovies you can buy, from a freshly opened tin or jar (see page 20). **Serves 4 to 6**

⅓ cup extra-virgin olive oil

10 large cloves garlic, coarsely chopped

8 anchovy fillets, minced to a paste

1½ pounds radicchio, quartered, cored, and coarsely chopped

Salt and freshly ground black pepper

1 pound spaghetti

6 tablespoons toasted bread crumbs (page 22)

Heat the olive oil in a very large skillet (at least 12 inches in diameter) over low heat. Add the garlic and cook slowly until it softens and just begins to color, about 15 minutes. Remove the skillet from the heat and add the anchovies. Stir with a wooden spoon until they dissolve.

Return the skillet to low heat and cook for 10 minutes to mellow the anchovy flavor, then add the radicchio. It will probably seem too much for the pan but will quickly cook down. Raise the heat to moderately low. Cook until the radicchio softens, about 10 minutes, stirring often so it cooks evenly. It should still have a touch of firmness; don't overcook it. Season with salt and pepper to taste.

Bring a large pot of salted water to a boil over high heat. Add the pasta and cook until al dente. Set aside 1 cup of the pasta water, then drain the pasta and return it to the warm pot over low heat. Add the sauce and toss well, moistening with some of the reserved pasta water as needed. Divide among warm bowls and top each portion with some of the bread crumbs. Serve immediately.

Orecchiette con Fagioli Freschi e Pomodoro

EAR-SHAPED PASTA WITH BUTTER BEANS AND TOMATO

The humble combination of pasta and beans is one of the most satisfying in Italy's pasta opus despite its obvious roots in deprivation and poverty. In my experience, few Americans understand the appeal of starch with starch, but to an Italian such dishes have the resonance of home. Pasta with beans is particularly commonplace in Puglia—see another Pugliese pasta-and-bean recipe on facing page—and beloved even in families with the resources to eat far more grandly. **Serves 4 to 6**

4 cups fresh shelled lima or cannellini beans, or other fresh shelling beans

½ yellow onion

1 celery rib, in 3 or 4 chunks

3 cloves garlic, one smashed and two minced

1 large fresh Italian (flat-leaf) parsley sprig, plus 2 tablespoons chopped

Salt

¼ cup extra-virgin olive oil, plus more for drizzling

½ teaspoon minced fresh rosemary

Pinch of hot pepper flakes

1 pound ripe plum tomatoes, grated (page 25)

1 pound orecchiette

Put the beans in a large saucepan with the onion, celery, smashed garlic, and parsley sprig. Add 5 cups water and bring to a simmer over moderately low heat. Partially cover and simmer until the beans are tender, 20 minutes or longer, depending on how dry they are. Season with salt to taste and let the beans cool in the liquid. Discard the onion, celery, garlic, and parsley. (You can prepare the beans to this point a day ahead.)

Heat the olive oil in a large skillet over moderately low heat. Add the minced garlic, chopped parsley, rosemary, and hot pepper flakes. Cook briefly to release the fragrance of the seasonings, then add the tomatoes. Bring to a simmer, season with salt to taste, and cook until the tomatoes soften and the sauce is smooth and flavorful, about 10 minutes. If the sauce threatens to cook dry before the tomatoes soften, add a little of the bean liquid.

Drain the beans, reserving the liquid. Add the beans to the tomato sauce, along with 1½ cups of the bean liquid. Cover and simmer gently for about 10 minutes to allow the beans to absorb the flavor of the sauce. Add more liquid if needed; the beans should be brothy.

Bring a large pot of salted water to a boil over high heat. Add the pasta and cook until about 2 minutes shy of al dente. Drain the pasta and return it to the warm pot over moderate heat. Add the sauce and cook, stirring, until the sauce thickens and cloaks the pasta nicely, about 2 minutes. If the sauce looks dry, add a little more bean liquid. Cover the pot and let stand for a couple of minutes, then divide among warm bowls. Drizzle each portion with additional olive oil before serving.

Cavatelli con Fagioli Freschi

BEAN-SHAPED PASTA WITH FRESH SHELL BEANS

You will probably have to visit a farmers' market to find fresh shell beans, or grow them yourself. They are one of the highlights of the late-summer harvest. Virtually any type will work in this recipe—cannellini, borlotti (also known as cranberry), limas, or black-eyed peas. If you can't find fresh beans, you can make the dish with dried beans, although you will have to soak them overnight and cook them longer.

I first had this pairing, served all over Puglia, at a restaurant in the southern Italian town of Trani. The kitchen used fresh cavatelli pasta and cannellini beans, which so resembled each other after cooking that you almost couldn't tell them apart—a delicious trompe l'oeil. This sauce has no tomato, so good olive oil really counts. **Serves 4 to 6**

3 cups fresh shelled cannellini or cranberry beans, or other fresh shelling beans

½ yellow onion

1 small celery rib, in large chunks

1 small carrot, in large chunks

2 cloves garlic, one smashed and one minced

1 large fresh Italian (flat-leaf) parsley sprig, plus 2 tablespoons chopped

Salt

1 pound cavatelli or gnocchetti sardi

3 tablespoons extra-virgin olive oil, plus more for drizzling

2 teaspoons chopped fresh sage

Pinch of hot pepper flakes

Put the beans in a large saucepan with the onion, celery, carrot, smashed garlic, and parsley sprig. Add 5 cups water and bring to a simmer over moderately low heat. Partially cover and simmer until the beans are tender, 20 minutes or longer, depending on how dry they are. Season with salt to taste and cool the beans in the liquid. Discard the onion, celery, carrot, garlic, and parsley. (You can prepare the beans to this point a day ahead.)

Bring a large pot of salted water to a boil over high heat. Add the pasta and cook until 1 minute shy of al dente. While the pasta is cooking, reheat the beans gently.

Combine the olive oil, minced garlic, 1 tablespoon of the chopped parsley, the sage, and the hot pepper flakes in a small skillet. Cook over moderately low heat just long enough to release the fragrance of the garlic and herbs.

Drain the pasta and return it to the warm pot. Add the seasoned oil and stir well. Add the beans with a slotted spoon, then add about ¹/₂ cup of the bean cooking liquid. Cook the pasta over moderately low heat for about 1 minute to allow the pasta to absorb some of the flavor of the sauce. Add a little more bean liquid if needed to moisten.

Serve in warm bowls, finishing each portion with a drizzle of olive oil and a sprinkle of the remaining 1 tablespoon chopped parsley.

Pasta Verde con Spinaci

SPINACH FETTUCCINE WITH SPINACH, BUTTER, AND PARMESAN

On several occasions, I've had the pleasure of writing about Paul Bertolli, the talented chef and partner at Oliveto restaurant in Oakland, California. Once, for a newspaper story, we went to the farmers' market together, and he shopped for an improvisational meal. Fresh spinach pasta tossed with spinach was one of his impromptu inventions, a dish I loved for its simplicity and pure taste. I have reproduced a variation here. **Serves 4 to 6**

Fresh Spinach Pasta (page 17), cut as fettuccine (page 18)

1½ to 2 pounds fresh spinach (not baby spinach), thick stems removed

5 tablespoons unsalted butter, in 10 pieces

Salt and freshly ground black pepper

⅔ cup freshly grated Parmesan cheese

Bring a large pot of salted water to a boil over high heat. Add the pasta and boil until it is about 1 minute shy of al dente. Add the spinach leaves and stir them down into the pot to wilt. When the spinach is completely wilted, set aside 1 cup of the pasta water, then drain the pasta and spinach and return them to the warm pot. Add the butter and salt and pepper to taste, then toss well. Add 1/2 cup of the cheese and toss again, moistening with some of the reserved pasta water as needed.

Divide among warm bowls, topping each portion with some of the remaining cheese. Serve immediately.

Cannelloni Ripieni di Spinaci

CANNELLONI WITH A FRESH SPINACH FILLING

Because of the time involved in making them, cannelloni are "weekends only" at my house. Start to finish, they take me two hours, but they're worth it. Recruiting a helper makes the project go much faster. I fill these with cooked spinach bound with béchamel, but you can use the same recipe as a template for a mushroom- or meat-filled version.

Alternatively, you can turn the same ingredients—noodles, spinach filling, and tomato sauce—into lasagne. Cut the pasta dough into long, wide noodles instead of into squares. Boil the noodles as directed for the squares, then layer the noodles in a baking dish with the spinach filling. Top with a thin layer of béchamel, all the tomato sauce, and a dusting of Parmesan, then bake as described for cannelloni.

I know many people think of cannelloni as a party dish because you can assemble them ahead, then bake as needed. Nevertheless, I wouldn't double or triple this recipe without kitchen assistance.

Serves 6

Fresh Egg Pasta (page 14) made with 2 extra-large eggs and approximately 1²⁄₃ cups unbleached all-purpose flour

For the Tomato Sauce:

2 tablespoons extra-virgin olive oil

1 large clove garlic, minced

Pinch of hot pepper flakes

2 cups grated ripe plum tomatoes (page 25)

12 fresh basil leaves, torn into small pieces

Salt

(continued)

Roll the pasta into thin sheets, one setting thinner than for fettuccine. (I roll to setting number 6.) Cut the sheets into 5- to 6-inch squares (depending on the width of your pasta machine's rollers); you should get at least 18 squares with some scraps. Arrange the pasta squares on clean dish towels and let them rest until you are ready to cook them.

To make the tomato sauce, heat the olive oil in a skillet over moderately low heat. Add the garlic and hot pepper flakes and cook briefly to release their fragrance. Add the tomatoes and basil and season with salt to taste. Simmer, stirring often, until the sauce thickens and reduces to about 1 cup. Set aside.

(continued)

CANNELLONI WITH A FRESH
SPINACH FILLING (CONTINUED)

For the Béchamel:

4 tablespoons unsalted butter

4 tablespoons unbleached all-purpose flour

3 cups whole milk

1 small bay leaf

1 clove garlic, halved

Salt and freshly ground black pepper

Freshly grated nutmeg

2 pounds fresh spinach

1 cup freshly grated Parmesan cheese

Salt and freshly ground black pepper

Unsalted butter for the baking dish

1 tablespoon olive oil

To make the béchamel, melt the butter in a saucepan over moderate heat. Add the flour and whisk to blend. Add the milk, whisking constantly. Add the bay leaf and garlic. Bring to a simmer, whisking often, then adjust the heat to cook at a bare simmer. Cook for 15 minutes, whisking often, then season with salt, pepper, and nutmeg to taste. Remove the bay leaf and garlic.

Meanwhile, wash the spinach and remove any thick stems. Put the spinach in a large pot with just the wash water clinging to it. Cover and cook over moderately high heat, tossing occasionally, until the spinach just wilts. Drain in a sieve and rinse with cold water to cool it quickly. Squeeze the spinach dry between your hands, then chop it fine.

Put the spinach in a bowl and add 1 1/2 cups of the béchamel and 1/2 cup of the cheese. Season with salt and pepper to taste and stir to blend.

Butter a baking dish large enough to hold 18 cannelloni arranged tightly side by side. Preheat the oven to 450°F.

Bring a large pot of salted water to a boil over high heat. Prepare a very large bowl of ice water; add the olive oil. Cook the pasta squares 2 at a time for 15 seconds only, then transfer them to the ice water. Immediately unfurl them with your hands to prevent them from sticking to each other.

Now you are ready to fill the cannelloni. Spread about $1/4$ cup of the béchamel in the baking dish to make a thin film. Arrange a clean dish towel on a work surface. Working with 1 pasta square at a time, lift it out of the ice water and transfer it to the dish towel. Pat it dry with another towel. Using a table knife, spread about 2 tablespoons of the spinach mixture on the square, keeping it away from the edges. Roll the square like a jelly roll to make a log about 1 inch wide and arrange seam side down in the baking dish. Continue with the remaining pasta squares, arranging the cannelloni closely side by side.

Top the cannelloni with béchamel, coating them evenly. (You may not need all the béchamel.) Spoon the tomato sauce on top, then spread it gently and evenly. Sprinkle the surface with the remaining $1/2$ cup cheese.

Bake until the cannelloni are bubbling hot, 15 to 20 minutes. Let cool 5 minutes before serving. To serve, use a spatula to lift them carefully out of the baking dish without cutting into them.

In the San Francisco Bay Area, where I live, several farmers' markets stay open year-round, and it always astounds me what farmers can coax from our cold, wet winter ground. The displays of hearty greens—collards, kale, dandelion greens, turnip greens, chard, and more—are prettier to me than the wares of any florist shop. And nothing is sadder than watching patrons walk right past, headed for the hothouse tomatoes and peppers.

Although not everyone has a farmers' market to draw from in winter, open-minded shoppers wherever they live will find their own market filled with potential for winter pasta sauces. Cabbage, that cold-weather mainstay, can be softened into a buttery sauce with onion and fennel seed. Cauliflower rises above the humble in a beloved Sicilian sauce with pine nuts, saffron, and currants. Broccoli rabe with orecchiette, on virtually every menu in Puglia, welcomes the addition of crumbled sausage or sweet turnips.

Dried beans should also be considered as part of the pasta cook's winter resources. The realm of Italian pasta-and-bean soups is virtually boundless, with ingredients and seasonings varying according to region and cook. I've chosen two favorites to showcase here: a northern-style recipe based on borlotti beans, and a southern variation with chickpeas, chile oil, and fresh semolina pasta.

winter recipes

LARGE PENNE WITH BROCCOLI, TOMATOES, AND CREAM

••

At the charming and simple La Gensola in Rome, I had a delightful lunch alone. First, the waiter assembled a platter of antipasti from the buffet for me, including eggplant prepared three different ways. This pasta dish followed, with nuggets of well-cooked broccoli in a luscious tomato sauce enriched, I suspect, with a touch of cream. **Serves 4 to 6**

••

2½ cups pureed fresh tomatoes (page 25) or 1 can (29 ounces) whole peeled tomatoes

1½ pounds broccoli, stems trimmed to 3 to 4 inches

¼ cup extra-virgin olive oil

4 large cloves garlic, minced

Pinch of hot pepper flakes

Salt

¼ cup heavy cream

1 pound pennone (large penne), penne rigate, or mezzi rigatoni

⅓ cup freshly grated Parmesan cheese, plus more for passing at the table

If using canned tomatoes, put the tomatoes and their juice through a food mill or puree in a blender and set aside.

Bring a large pot of salted water to a boil over high heat. Pare the broccoli stems with a small knife, removing the tough outer layer, then slit the stems lengthwise so they cook more quickly. Boil until tender but not soggy, 5 to 7 minutes. Transfer the broccoli to a sieve with tongs and cool under cold running water. Drain well and chop coarsely.

Add 1 cup water to the pot and return to a boil.

Heat the olive oil in a large skillet over moderately low heat. Add the garlic and hot pepper flakes and sauté briefly to release the garlic fragrance. Add the pureed tomato, season with salt to taste, and bring to a simmer. Adjust the heat to maintain a gentle simmer and cook, stirring often, until the sauce is thick and flavorful, about 20 minutes. Stir in the cream and broccoli and reduce the heat to low. Cook the broccoli gently in the sauce while you cook the pasta.

Add the pasta to the boiling water and cook until al dente. Set aside 1 cup of the pasta water, then drain the pasta and return it to the warm pot over low heat. Add the sauce and toss well, moistening with some of the reserved pasta water as needed. Add the cheese and toss again. Serve immediately in warm bowls. Pass the additional cheese at the table.

EAR-SHAPED PASTA WITH TURNIPS, BROCCOLI RABE, AND HOT PEPPER FLAKES

• •

A few grandmothers still make orecchiette by hand for Sunday lunch in Puglia, the southern Italian region where this ear-shaped pasta is a specialty. Unfortunately, few young people know how to do it, and most buy their orecchiette dried in a box or fresh at a local pasta shop. Broccoli rabe is the most common accompaniment for this shape. You'd have to look hard to find a Pugliese restaurant without *orecchiette alle cime di rapa*—pasta with broccoli rabe—on the menu.

In times past, broccoli rabe was probably a foraged wild green in Italy, not a cultivated vegetable. Edward Giobbi, the Italian-American cookbook author, says that old Italian cookbooks don't mention the vegetable. In this country, broccoli rabe was largely relegated to markets in Italian neighborhoods until the 1990s, when Americans began to embrace the southern Italian kitchen. Now D'Arrigo Brothers in Salinas, California, the largest broccoli rabe grower and shipper in the country, supplies the vegetable to markets everywhere, grown from proprietary seed that the company has worked for years to perfect.

Although I've never seen this combination in Puglia, I think sweet turnips—which are a broccoli rabe relative—are an appealing counterpoint to the pleasantly bitter rabe. **Serves 4 to 6**

• •

¾ pound small, young turnips

1¼ to 1½ pounds broccoli rabe

6 tablespoons extra-virgin olive oil

Salt

4 cloves garlic, minced

¼ teaspoon hot pepper flakes

1 pound orecchiette

Freshly grated aged pecorino cheese (optional)

Bring a large pot of salted water to a boil over high heat.

Peel the turnips thickly and cut into bite-sized cubes. To trim the broccoli rabe, remove any stems that feel tough. (The thick stems are usually more tender than the thin ones.) Trim the ends of any stems that look dry, then slit any stems that are thicker than a pencil so they cook more quickly.

Heat 1 tablespoon of the olive oil in a large skillet over moderately high heat. Add the turnips, season with salt to taste, and toss to coat with the oil. Cook briskly until the turnips are nicely colored all over, about 5 minutes. If they are still underdone, cover the skillet, reduce the heat to low, and let them steam until they are barely tender. Add another 1 tablespoon of the olive oil, the garlic, and the hot pepper flakes. Cook about 1 minute to release the garlic fragrance. Set the skillet aside.

Add the broccoli rabe to the boiling water and cook until the stems are just tender, about 3 minutes. Using tongs, transfer the broccoli rabe to a sieve and cool quickly under cold running water. (Keep the cooking water at a boil.) Drain the broccoli rabe well, then squeeze gently to remove excess water. Chop coarsely.

Add the pasta to the boiling water and cook until al dente. While the pasta is cooking, add the broccoli rabe and the remaining 4 tablespoons olive oil to the skillet with the turnips. Season generously with salt and reheat gently.

Set aside 1 cup of the pasta water, then drain the pasta and return it to the warm pot over low heat. Add the sauce and toss well, moistening with some of the reserved pasta water as needed. Divide among warm bowls and serve immediately. Pass the cheese at the table for those who want it.

EAR-SHAPED PASTA WITH BROCCOLI RABE AND SAUSAGE

This pasta dish from Puglia is my fallback position, the one-pot dinner I turn to when I'm too tired and hungry to contemplate something more ambitious.

I have read many recipes for orecchiette with broccoli rabe—it is Puglia's signature dish—and watched Pugliese cooks make it. Typically, in a nod to efficiency, they boil the vegetable along with the pasta, but that always results in soggy broccoli rabe. The dish is vastly improved if you boil the rabe first, squeeze out excess moisture, and then reheat it with olive oil and seasonings. Some recipes instruct you to remove the thick stems of broccoli rabe, but the thick stems are tender. It's the thin, stringy stems that can be tough. **Serves 4 to 6**

1½ to 2 pounds broccoli rabe

1 pound orecchiette or spaghetti

6 tablespoons extra-virgin olive oil

4 large cloves garlic, minced

Pinch of hot pepper flakes

6 to 8 ounces hot Italian sausage, preferably with fennel seed

Salt

Freshly grated aged pecorino cheese (optional)

Bring a large pot of salted water to a boil over high heat. To trim the broccoli rabe, remove any stems that feel tough. (The thick stems are usually more tender than the thin ones.) Trim the ends of any stems that look dry, then slit any stems that are thicker than a pencil so they cook more quickly. Add the broccoli rabe to the boiling water and cook until the stems are just tender, about 3 minutes. Using tongs, transfer the broccoli rabe to a sieve and cool quickly under cold running water. (Keep the cooking water at a boil.) Drain well, then squeeze gently to remove excess water. Chop coarsely.

Add the pasta to the boiling water and cook until al dente.

While the pasta is cooking, put the olive oil, garlic, and hot pepper flakes in a large skillet. Remove the sausage from its casing if necessary and add it to the cold skillet. Warm over moderately low heat, breaking up the sausage with a fork, and cook just until the sausage loses most of its pinkness. Add the broccoli rabe and season with salt to taste. Stir to coat with the seasonings and reheat gently.

Set aside 1 cup of the pasta water, then drain the pasta and return it to the warm pot over low heat. Add the sauce and toss well, moistening with some of the reserved pasta water as needed. Divide among warm bowls and serve immediately. Pass the cheese at the table for those who want it.

WHOLE-WHEAT PASTA WITH BRAISED SAVOY CABBAGE AND FENNEL SEED

Whole-wheat pasta has a robust, nutty, grainy taste that I like with winter greens and cabbage. The pasta's texture suffers a little because whole wheat contains the bran, which cuts the gluten strands created when dough is kneaded. That's why whole-wheat pasta is not as firm to the tooth as pasta from refined flour. My husband dislikes it for that reason, so I cook it for myself when he's away.

You could add a little crumbled sausage to this sauce if you like, but it doesn't need it. If you can't find whole-wheat fusilli (De Cecco makes it), substitute another whole-wheat shape, or use regular fusilli. **Serves 4 to 6**

6 tablespoons unsalted butter

1 large yellow onion, minced

3 large cloves garlic, minced

Pinch of hot pepper flakes

2 pounds Savoy cabbage, halved, then cut into 1-inch wedges, cored, and thinly sliced crosswise

¾ teaspoon fennel seed, crushed in a mortar or spice grinder

Salt

2 tablespoons minced fresh Italian (flat-leaf) parsley

1 pound whole-wheat fusilli or other short dried pasta

½ cup freshly grated Parmesan cheese, plus more for passing at the table

Melt 4 tablespoons of the butter in a large skillet over moderately low heat. Add the onion and sauté until soft and starting to color, about 10 minutes. Add the garlic and hot pepper flakes and sauté briefly to release the garlic fragrance. Add the cabbage and fennel seed, season with salt to taste, and stir well. Cover and cook, stirring occasionally, until the cabbage wilts and softens, about 20 minutes. Taste and adjust the seasoning. Stir in the parsley and keep warm.

Bring a large pot of salted water to a boil over high heat. Add the pasta and cook until al dente. Set aside 1 cup of the pasta water, then drain the pasta and return it to the warm pot over low heat. Add the cabbage, the remaining 2 tablespoons butter, and the cheese. Toss until the butter melts, moistening with reserved pasta water—you will probably need quite a bit of it.

Divide the pasta among warm bowls and serve immediately. Pass the additional cheese at the table.

LONG PIERCED PASTA WITH CAULIFLOWER, PINE NUTS, CURRANTS, AND SAFFRON

This exotic combination is pure Sicilian and surely the most common Sicilian way of preparing pasta with cauliflower. (Confusingly, *broccoli* is cauliflower in Sicily.) Pine nuts and currants are used together in so many Sicilian dishes that markets sell them already combined, and recipes routinely call for *passoline e pinoli* as if they were one ingredient. For that reason, it's probably safe to say that most Sicilian cooks don't plump their currants or toast their pine nuts for this dish, but I think both are worth doing.

It's always a challenge to specify an accurate quantity of saffron threads because they are awkward to measure. My approach is to pack them lightly into a measuring spoon and to err on the light side. You can always add more later, but too much saffron can ruin a dish. **Serves 4 to 6**

Generous ⅛ teaspoon saffron threads, or more if needed

3 tablespoons currants or golden raisins

1 cauliflower, 1½ to 1¾ pounds

6 tablespoons extra-virgin olive oil

1 yellow onion, finely minced

Generous pinch of hot pepper flakes

Salt

8 anchovy fillets, minced to a paste

3 tablespoons toasted pine nuts (page 24)

2 tablespoons minced fresh Italian (flat-leaf) parsley

1 pound bucatini (perciatelli) or spaghetti

½ cup toasted bread crumbs (page 22) (optional)

Soak the saffron threads in 2 tablespoons water for at least 20 minutes to allow their flavor to bloom. Plump the currants in 3 tablespoons warm water for about 20 minutes.

Bring a large pot of salted water to a boil over high heat. Trim the cauliflower, removing any leaves and separating the florets from the stems. Try to leave the florets in large clusters so they don't get soggy when cooked.

Add the cauliflower to the boiling water and cook until barely tender when pierced, about 5 minutes. Lift the florets out of the boiling water with tongs or a skimmer. (Keep the cooking water at a boil.) Let the cauliflower cool, then chop coarsely; you should still have some large pieces.

Heat the olive oil in a large skillet over moderately low heat. Add the onion and hot pepper flakes and sauté until the onion is soft, about 10 minutes. Add the saffron and its water and the currants with their soaking liquid. Simmer gently for a couple of minutes to flavor the onion base, then add the cauliflower. Season with salt to taste and stir to coat with the seasonings. Cover and simmer briefly to infuse the cauliflower with the seasonings, but take care not to overcook it; the cauliflower should be tender but not mushy. Add a few tablespoons of the boiling water if the sauce looks dry. If the saffron flavor does not seem strong enough, infuse a few more threads in a little of the hot pasta water for a minute or two, then add to the skillet.

Stir in the anchovies, pine nuts, and parsley. Keep the sauce warm over low heat.

Add the pasta to the boiling water and cook until al dente. Set aside 1 cup of the pasta water, then drain the pasta and return it to the warm pot over low heat. Add the sauce and toss well, moistening with some of the reserved pasta water as needed. Divide among warm bowls. Pass the bread crumbs at the table for those who want them.

EAR-SHAPED PASTA WITH CAULIFLOWER, ONIONS, PANCETTA, AND PECORINO

After broccoli rabe, cauliflower is probably the vegetable paired most often with orecchiette in Puglia. Sometimes it's simmered in tomato sauce, or enhanced with anchovies and bread crumbs. Sometimes it's seasoned only with garlic and dried chile. I particularly like it with pancetta, softened onions, and a shower of sharp pecorino. **Serves 4 to 6**

1 large cauliflower, about 2 pounds

6 tablespoons extra-virgin olive oil

1 yellow onion, minced

¼ pound pancetta, minced

4 cloves garlic, minced

¼ cup minced fresh Italian (flat-leaf) parsley

Salt and freshly ground black pepper

1 pound orecchiette

½ cup freshly grated aged pecorino cheese

Bring a large pot of salted water to a boil over high heat. Trim the cauliflower, removing any leaves and separating the florets from the stem. Try to leave the florets in large clusters so they don't get soggy when cooked.

Add the cauliflower to the boiling water and cook, uncovered, until tender when pierced, 8 to 10 minutes. Lift the florets out of the boiling water with tongs or a skimmer. Let them cool, then chop them; there should be no large pieces. Add another 1 cup water to the pot and return to a boil.

Put the olive oil, onion, pancetta, garlic, and parsley in a large skillet and cook over moderate heat, stirring occasionally, until the onion is soft, about 10 minutes. Add the chopped cauliflower, season generously with salt, and stir well. Reduce the heat to low and let the cauliflower cook gently while you cook the pasta.

Add the pasta to the boiling water and cook until al dente. Set aside 1 cup of the pasta water, then drain the pasta and return it to the warm pot over low heat. Add the sauce and toss, moistening with some of the reserved pasta water if needed. Add the cheese and several grinds of black pepper and toss again. Serve immediately in warm bowls.

PENNE WITH MUSTARD GREENS, RICOTTA, AND PECORINO

· ·

During a short stay at Regaleali, the delightful Sicilian wine estate, I tasted the pasta dish that inspired this one. Proprietor Anna Tasca Lanza, a cookbook author herself, made it with spaghetti, wild mustard greens, and the fresh sheep's-milk ricotta made on the estate, all gently tossed together with good olive oil, garlic, and a handful of grated pecorino.

Because neither the wild greens nor the sheep's-milk ricotta is available to most Americans, I decided to put my own stamp on Anna's recipe. This modified version, using store-bought mustard greens and our creamier cow's-milk ricotta, departs significantly from Anna's approach but is no less delicious. **Serves 4 to 6**

· ·

1½ to 1¾ pounds mustard greens, central ribs removed

1 pound penne rigate

⅓ cup extra-virgin olive oil

4 large cloves garlic, minced

Pinch of hot pepper flakes

Salt and freshly ground black pepper

10 ounces whole-milk ricotta, at room temperature

¾ cup freshly grated aged pecorino cheese

Put a serving bowl in a low oven to warm.

Bring a large pot of salted water to a boil over high heat. Add the mustard greens, pushing them down into the water with tongs, and boil until tender, about 5 minutes. Transfer them to a sieve with the tongs or a skimmer and cool quickly under cold running water. (Keep the cooking water at a boil.) Squeeze the greens gently to remove excess water, but leave them moist. Chop coarsely.

Add the pasta to the boiling water and cook until al dente.

While the pasta is cooking, heat the olive oil in a large skillet over moderately low heat. Add the garlic and hot pepper flakes and sauté briefly to release the garlic fragrance. Add the mustard greens and season with salt to taste. Stir to coat with the seasonings and cook until the mustard greens are hot. Moisten if needed with some of the boiling pasta water; the greens should not be dry.

In a bowl, combine the ricotta and pecorino and stir until smooth. Season with salt and pepper to taste.

Just before the pasta is done, remove the serving bowl from the oven. Put the seasoned cheese in the bowl and whisk in enough of the hot pasta water to make a creamy sauce. Set aside 1 more cup of the pasta water, then drain the pasta and transfer it to the bowl. Toss well to coat with the cheese sauce, moistening if needed with some of the reserved pasta water. Divide the pasta among warm bowls and top each portion with some of the mustard greens. Serve immediately.

SPAGHETTI WITH TUSCAN KALE, SAUSAGE, TOMATOES, AND PARMESAN

· ·

The deep blue-green, crinkled Tuscan kale—also known as dinosaur kale, *lacinato* kale, and *cavolo nero*, its Italian name—is far more tender and delicious than the curly kale most supermarkets carry. This recipe will work with whatever type of kale you can find, but I encourage you to look for Tuscan kale or try to grow it. See Resources (page 123) for seed sources. It is easy to grow and provides a nutritious harvest for many weeks. **Serves 4 to 6**

· ·

⅓ to ½ pound hot Italian sausage, preferably with fennel seed

⅓ cup extra-virgin olive oil

4 cloves garlic, minced

¼ teaspoon hot pepper flakes, or to taste

One 14½-ounce can whole plum tomatoes

Salt

¾ pound kale, preferably Tuscan kale, central ribs removed

1 pound spaghetti

⅓ cup freshly grated Parmesan cheese, plus more for garnish and for passing at the table

Bring a large pot of salted water to a boil over high heat.

Remove the sausage casings if necessary and put the sausage in a large cold skillet with the olive oil. Heat over moderately low heat, breaking up the sausage with a fork, and cook just until the sausage loses most of its pinkness. Add the garlic and hot pepper flakes and cook for a minute or two to release their fragrance. Add the juices from the tomato can, then crush the tomatoes between your fingers directly into the skillet.

Adjust the heat to maintain a gentle simmer and cook, stirring often, until the sauce thickens, about 15 minutes. Season with salt to taste.

Add the kale to the boiling water, pushing it down into the water with tongs. Cook until tender, about 5 minutes. Transfer to a sieve with the tongs and cool quickly under cold running water. (Keep the cooking water at a boil.) Drain the kale well, then squeeze gently to remove excess water. Chop coarsely. Add the kale to the skillet and stir well.

Add the pasta to the boiling water and cook until al dente. Set aside 1 cup of the hot pasta water, then drain the pasta and return it to the warm pot over low heat. Add the sauce and toss well, moistening with some of the reserved pasta water if needed. Add the cheese and toss again. Divide among warm bowls, top each portion with a little additional grated cheese, and serve immediately. Pass more cheese at the table.

LONG PIERCED PASTA WITH A WINTER KALE AND WALNUT PESTO

When fresh basil is out of season, you can make an alternative pesto with the sweet, nutty Tuscan kale that is increasingly available in produce markets (see facing page). It works better than common curly kale in this recipe because it's more tender and mild. If you can't find it, you can use curly kale, but the taste will be stronger.

I try to rub off as much of the toasted walnut skins as possible so the sauce won't taste tannic. I also use some of my best extra-virgin olive oil for at least half of the olive oil required.

You may have leftover pesto, depending on how generously you like to sauce your pasta. Serve it on crostini or polenta the next day. **Serves 4 to 6**

½ pound kale, preferably Tuscan kale, central ribs removed

2 large cloves garlic

Scant ½ cup walnuts, toasted (page 24)

½ cup plus 2 tablespoons extra-virgin olive oil

⅓ cup freshly grated Parmesan cheese, plus more for garnish

Salt

1 pound bucatini (perciatelli) or spaghetti

Bring a large pot of salted water to a boil over high heat. Add the kale, pushing it down into the water with tongs, and cook until tender, 3 to 5 minutes or longer depending on its age and type. Transfer to a sieve with the tongs and cool quickly under cold running water. (Keep the cooking water at a boil.) Drain the kale, then squeeze gently to remove excess water.

Put the kale in a food processor with the garlic and walnuts and process until nearly smooth. With the machine running, add the olive oil gradually until the pesto is creamy; it doesn't need to be completely smooth. Transfer the pesto to a bowl and stir in the cheese, then season generously with salt.

Add the pasta to the boiling water and cook until al dente. Just before the pasta is done, whisk enough of the hot pasta water into the pesto to make a thin sauce, about 1/2 cup.

Set aside 1 cup of the pasta water, then drain the pasta and return it to the warm pot. Add as much of the pesto as you need to coat the pasta, then toss well, moistening with some of the reserved pasta water as needed. Divide among warm bowls and top each portion with a little additional cheese.

SOUP OF SEMOLINA PASTA, CHICKPEAS, TOMATOES, OREGANO, AND CHILE OIL

Some of the pasta-and-bean soups I've most enjoyed in Italy have had fresh pasta in them, not dried. This version, my re-creation of a soup I recall from the Molise region, includes fresh semolina noodles stretched with a rolling pin. The dough is a pleasure to work with, and the satisfaction of stretching your own pasta by hand repays the modest effort.

In the Molise and neighboring Abruzzo, hearty soups such as this one often arrive at the table with *diavolicchio*, a chile-oil condiment that the diner adds to taste. It is easy to make at home with dried red chiles and will keep, refrigerated, for several weeks. The dried oregano should have a lively fragrance; if yours is more than 6 months old, you should replace it. **Serves 4**

For the Chile Oil:

2 small hot dried red chiles, or 1 teaspoon hot pepper flakes, or to taste

½ cup extra-virgin olive oil

1 cup chickpeas, soaked overnight in water to cover

½ yellow onion

1 bay leaf

Salt

¼ cup extra-virgin olive oil

3 large cloves garlic, minced

Generous pinch of hot pepper flakes

¾ cup pureed fresh tomato (page 25)

1½ teaspoons dried oregano

To make the Chile Oil: Put the dried chiles, if using, in a spice mill and grind until well chopped. Put the chopped chiles or hot pepper flakes in a small bowl and add the olive oil. Cover and let stand at room temperature for 2 days. The oil should become tinged with chile color.

Drain and rinse the chickpeas. Transfer them to a large pot and add 2 quarts cold water, the onion, and the bay leaf. Bring to a simmer over moderately low heat, skimming any foam. Cover and adjust the heat to maintain a gentle simmer. Cook until the chickpeas are tender, 1 hour or longer, depending on age. Season with salt to taste and let the beans cool in the liquid. Remove the onion and bay leaf. (You can cook the chickpeas 1 or 2 days ahead.)

Heat the olive oil in a skillet over moderately low heat. Add the garlic and hot pepper flakes and cook briefly to release the garlic fragrance. Add the tomato and oregano, crushing the herb between your fingers. Season with salt to taste and cook, stirring, until the mixture comes together into a sauce, 3 to 5 minutes. Add the sauce to the chickpeas. (You can prepare the chickpeas and sauce to this point several hours or 1 day ahead.)

For the Semolina Pasta:

Scant 1 cup semolina, plus more for kneading

Pinch of salt

Unbleached all-purpose flour for dusting

To make the pasta, put the semolina and salt in a bowl and stir to blend. Add $1/3$ cup water and stir until the mixture begins to come together. Use your hand to collect the dough into a ball, then transfer it to a work surface. Knead until the dough is smooth and no longer sticky or grainy, dusting the work surface with semolina as needed.

Discard any semolina remaining on the work surface and dust the surface with flour. Working with a rolling pin, stretch the dough into a ribbon 6 to 7 inches wide and at least 3 feet long. If you can make it longer, so much the better, as the noodles will be thinner, but don't make it wider. Flour the dough lightly on both sides as needed to prevent sticking.

With a pastry wheel, cut the dough in half lengthwise, then cut crosswise into short noodles about $1/2$ inch wide. Let the noodles dry on dish towels for at least 4 hours.

To finish the dish, bring the chickpeas to a simmer over moderately high heat. Add the pasta, stir well, cover, and adjust the heat to maintain a gentle simmer. Cook until the pasta is al dente, about 5 minutes, stirring often to prevent the noodles from sticking to each other and adding boiling water if needed to thin the broth. The dish should be brothy, not thick. Taste and adjust the seasoning. Remove from the heat and let stand for 5 minutes before serving. Serve in warm bowls. Pass the chile oil for each diner to add to taste.

BORLOTTI BEAN AND VEGETABLE SOUP WITH PASTA, PANCETTA, AND ROSEMARY

Some of Italy's most satisfying dishes come out of rural peasant kitchens, where people have had to figure out how to make much from a little. The country's repertoire of pasta-and-bean soups reflects this resourceful spirit: With provisions from the pantry and a winter vegetable or two, good cooks create sturdy soups that provide enormous pleasure. If you can't find borlotti beans, also known as cranberry beans, use cannellini beans. **Serves 6**

1½ cups dried borlotti (cranberry) beans, soaked overnight in water to cover

3 tablespoons extra-virgin olive oil, plus more for drizzling

3 ounces pancetta, minced

½ yellow onion, minced

2 large cloves garlic, minced

1½ tablespoons minced fresh rosemary

1 tablespoon minced fresh sage

2 celery ribs, in ½-inch dice

1 large carrot, in ½-inch dice

¾ pound russet (baking) potato, peeled, in ½-inch dice

Salt and freshly ground black pepper

½ pound small soup pasta, such as ditali or tubetti

Drain the beans.

Heat the olive oil and pancetta in a large pot over moderately low heat. Cook until the pancetta renders some of its fat and begins to crisp. Add the onion, garlic, rosemary, and sage. Cook until the onion is soft, about 10 minutes. Add the beans, celery, carrot, potato, and 2 quarts cold water. Bring to a simmer, stirring occasionally. Cover and adjust the heat to maintain a gentle simmer. Cook until the beans are tender, about 1 hour.

With a slotted spoon, transfer about 4 cups of the beans and vegetables to a food processor, leaving the broth in the pot. Add enough broth to the food processor to make a puree, then process until smooth. Return the puree to the pot. Stir well and season with salt and pepper to taste.

Bring the soup to a simmer over moderate heat. Add the pasta, cover, and adjust the heat to maintain a gentle simmer. Cook until the pasta is barely al dente. Remove from the heat and let stand, covered, for 10 minutes before serving. Serve in warm bowls, drizzling each portion with extra-virgin olive oil.

Tubetti con Ceci e Cicoria

SMALL PASTA TUBES WITH CHICKPEAS, ESCAROLE, AND PANCETTA

When I buy escarole for winter salads, I look for heavy heads with lots of crisp, blanched heart. The dark green outer leaves are too tough for salad, but I never throw them away. I save them until the next day, then blanch them and reheat them with olive oil and garlic, or use them in pasta sauces.

Canned chickpeas have good texture and flavor, and I don't consider them a compromise. (Avoid the bland low-sodium versions.) Enhanced with pancetta, onion, garlic, and rosemary, then simmered a few minutes with pasta and escarole, they make an easy and nourishing dinner. Get out your best olive oil for the final flourish. **Serves 4 to 6**

¼ cup extra-virgin olive oil, plus more for drizzling

¼ pound pancetta, minced

1 red onion, minced

2 large cloves garlic, minced

Pinch of hot pepper flakes

Two 15½-ounce cans chickpeas (not low sodium), with their liquid

One 4-inch sprig fresh rosemary

Salt

2 large heads escarole

1 pound tubetti (ditali) or other small dried pasta

Heat the olive oil and pancetta in a large skillet over moderately low heat and cook until the pancetta begins to crisp, about 10 minutes. Add the onion and cook until soft, about 10 minutes. Add the garlic and hot pepper flakes and cook briefly to release their fragrance. Add the chickpeas, including their liquid, and the rosemary sprig. Bring to a simmer, cover, and adjust the heat to maintain a gentle simmer. Cook until the chickpeas are bathed in a flavorful sauce, about 10 minutes. Check occasionally and remove the rosemary sprig when the flavor is strong enough. Season with salt to taste. Keep warm.

Bring a large pot of salted water to a boil over high heat. Separate the escarole heads into individual leaves. Reserve the pale tender hearts for salad. Add the other leaves to the boiling water, pushing them down into the water with tongs. Cook for 2 minutes, then transfer them with the tongs to a sieve and cool quickly under cold running water. (Keep the cooking water at a boil.) Drain the escarole well, then squeeze gently to remove excess water. Chop coarsely.

Add the pasta to the boiling water and cook until about 2 minutes shy of al dente. Set aside 1 cup of the pasta water, then drain the pasta and return it to the warm pot over moderately low heat. Add the chickpeas and the escarole. Cover and cook, stirring occasionally, until the pasta is al dente, 3 to 4 minutes longer. Moisten with some of the reserved pasta water as needed. Remove from the heat and let stand, covered, for about 5 minutes. Serve in warm bowls, drizzling a generous amount of olive oil over each portion.

For pasta-making equipment, including KitchenAid pasta attachments:

Fante's Kitchen Wares Shop
1006 S. Ninth Street
Philadelphia, PA 19147
800-44-FANTE
www.fantes.com

For pizzichi (short, wide farro pasta):

Market Hall Foods
888-952-4005

For Sicilian dried oregano:

A. G. Ferrari Foods
877-878-2783
www.agferrari.com

For Tuscan kale seeds:

Johnny's Selected Seeds
955 Benton Avenue
Winslow, ME 04901
207-861-3900
www.johnnyseeds.com

Nichols Garden Nursery
1190 Old Salem Road NE
Albany, OR 97321
800-422-3985
www.nicholsgardennursery.com

For Calabrian chiles in olive oil:

Vivande Porta Via
2125 Fillmore Street
San Francisco, CA 94115
415-346-4430
www.vivande.com

For oil-packed or salt-packed Agostino Recca anchovies:

Market Hall Foods
888-952-4005

For other Italian specialty foods, such as pasta (De Cecco, Rustichella, Martelli, and Latini), salt-packed capers, canned tomatoes, dried cannellini or borlotti beans, and dried porcini:

A. G. Ferrari Foods
877-878-2783
www.agferrari.com

Market Hall Foods
888-952-4005

Vivande Porta Via
2125 Fillmore Street
San Francisco, CA 94115
415-346-4430
www.vivande.com

BIBLIOGRAPHY

The following books have been helpful to me in preparing this manuscript.

Adda, Mario. *The Land of Olive Trees: A Food and Wine Guide to Apulia.*
Translated by Kevin Wren and Elena Palazzo. Bari: Mario Adda Editore, 1993.

Bugialli, Giuliano. *Bugialli on Pasta.*
New York: Simon and Schuster, 1988.

Conti, Mariella. *La pasta siciliana.*
Santa Venerina: Brancato Editore, 2000.

Del Conte, Anna. *Portrait of Pasta.*
New York: Paddington Press, 1976.

Frusteri, Leonardo, Salvatore Fraterrigo, Alba Allotta, and Paolo Salerno. *I tesori della cucina siciliana.*
Trapani: PS Advert Edizioni, 2002.

Gosetti, Fernanda. *Primi piatti della cucina regionale italiana.*
Milan: Fabbri Editori, 1989.

Plotkin, Fred. *The Authentic Pasta Book.*
New York: Simon and Schuster, 1985.

Scott, Maria Luisa, and Jack Denton Scott. *The New Complete Book of Pasta.*
New York: William Morrow and Company, 1985.

INDEX

The exact equivalents in the following tables have been rounded for convenience.

Liquid/Dry Measures

U.S.	Metric
¼ teaspoon	1.25 milliliters
½ teaspoon	2.5 milliliters
1 teaspoon	5 milliliters
1 tablespoon (3 teaspoons)	15 milliliters
1 fluid ounce (2 tablespoons)	30 milliliters
¼ cup	60 milliliters
⅓ cup	80 milliliters
½ cup	120 milliliters
1 cup	240 milliliters
1 pint (2 cups)	480 milliliters
1 quart (4 cups, 32 ounces)	960 milliliters
1 gallon (4 quarts)	3.84 liters
1 ounce (by weight)	28 grams
1 pound	454 grams
2.2 pounds	1 kilogram

Length

U.S.	Metric
⅛ inch	3 millimeters
¼ inch	6 millimeters
½ inch	12 millimeters
1 inch	2.5 centimeters

Oven Temperature

Fahrenheit	Celsius	Gas
250	120	½
275	140	1
300	150	2
325	160	3
350	180	4
375	190	5
400	200	6
425	220	7
450	230	8
475	240	9
500	260	10

NOTES